All about the Movies

Author, at age twenty-five, using a portable typewriter to do some work at home in early 1940.

All about the Movies

A Handbook for the Movie-Loving Layman

Maurice Rapf

The Scarecrow Press, Inc.
Lanham, Maryland, and London
2000

SCARECROW PRESS, INC.

Published in the United States of America
by Scarecrow Press, Inc.
4720 Boston Way, Lanham, Maryland 20706
http://www.scarecrowpress.com

4 Pleydell Gardens, Folkestone
Kent CT20 2DN, England

British Library Cataloguing in Publication Information Available

Library of Congress Cataloging-in-Publication Data

Rapf, Maurice, 1914–
    All about the movies : a handbook for the movie-loving layman /
Maurice Rapf.
        p. cm.
    Includes bibliographical references and index.
    ISBN 0-8108-3768-4 (alk. paper)–ISBN 0-8108-3791-9 (pbk. : alk. paper)
        1. Motion pictures. I. Title

PN1994.R28 2000
791.43—dc21   00-026520

Contents

Introduction

People everywhere love the movies and, as the wise comedian–actor Will Rogers once said, "Everyone has two businesses—his own and the movies." For my part, I have been teaching courses in film studies for thirty years. When I began in 1966, it was not easy to convince academic committees (whose approval was required) that courses in film studies belonged in a college or university curriculum. "Courses in film," the committee members said to justify their disapproval, "are not backed by any significant body of literature." To which an advocate of a film course replied, "There certainly is a body of literature, but it's all in cans."

Canned literature or not, the first film course at Dartmouth College—a history of film taught by Arthur Mayer, a Harvard graduate with no advanced degrees—was introduced in 1964 as a seminar that did not require approval by an academic committee. It proved so popular that I was brought to the Dartmouth campus two years later as a replacement for Mayer, who had already passed his eightieth birthday.

Hiring me proved to be a futile gesture; no one could replace Mayer. He had been involved with the movie business since 1912, as publicist, theater owner, and producer, and he had known personally almost all the major figures in movie history. Besides, he was a remarkable raconteur, and if some of his anecdotes were apocryphal, they were at the very least informative and entertaining. I never replaced him; he continued to teach the film history course until ill health forced him to retire at ninety-one. In the meanwhile, I stayed on to teach some film courses of my own, ultimately becoming director of what would be known as the Film Studies Program in the Drama Department.

Today there is no dearth of literature about the movies. Almost any reputable bookstore has hundreds of movie books on hand—history, theory, criticism, biographies, how to write screenplays, how to shoot, how to light, how to edit, how to arrange financing. Name any aspect of the movie business and you'll probably find at least a dozen books that deal with it. Since few people read even a smattering of the thousands of books about the movies that are now available, this book is an attempt to fill in some of the information that movie lovers should have but usually don't. It does not repeat the information that is dished out on *Entertainment Tonight, Hard Copy,* or *Access Hollywood,* but it focuses on the nitty-gritty—the modus vivendi of a medium that is just now celebrating its one-hundredth anniversary.

My connection with the industry doesn't quite add up to that centennial mark, but it comes close. It began during World War I, when my father, Harry Rapf, augmented his career in vaudeville by producing feature movies. Between the ages of three and ten I appeared in many of his movies as a scruffy child actor.

My father always had a penchant for movies about kids and animals. One of his early stars was a freckled-faced youngster named Wesley Barry. I appeared in most of Barry's movies as an extra or playing bits for the simple reason that, in those days before unionization, I came cheap. I remember one film called *School Days* (1921) in which I appear first as a classmate of Barry's in a one-room country schoolhouse. When he is taken to the city by his hoity-toity relatives, I appear as a classmate of his in a tony private school—this time wearing a little velvet suit and an Eton collar.

Thus I grew up in the movie business, moving to Hollywood when my father migrated west in 1921. I had three or four Rin Tin Tin puppies when my father started making Rin Tin Tin pictures for Warner Bros. with great success. The huge M-G-M lot became my playground when my father joined that new company as a vice president in 1924.

My father thought I should learn the business from the ground up, so, starting at the age of ten, I worked at M-G-M each summer. I was an office boy, then an assistant editor, a lab technician, an assistant soundman, a researcher, a reader, and, finally, after graduation from college, a junior writer. I never assumed the studio-executive position for which I was being groomed. Somewhere along the road to education I turned left and found myself blacklisted as an alleged Communist. I had to leave Hollywood altogether and found work in New York on what are known as "sponsored" films. Ultimately I became a teacher of film studies at Dartmouth.

I never intended to write a book about various aspects of the movies or about how they are made. Not that I think the subject has been thoroughly covered—I am always amazed at how little movie lovers know about the moviemaking process. But maybe that's just as well, since they suspend their disbelief when they go to the movies; they want to see a story unfold as if it were true (even the romance of Jack and Rose aboard the ill-fated *Titanic*). If the actors and actresses are well-known and have appeared in a variety of troublesome situations, the moviegoer watches their trials and tribulations as if they were drawn from life itself or, if it be comedy, as if the fun and games were only a mild distortion of recognized reality. If the illustrious performers don't actually make up their meaningful or witty lines, who cares who did? If the villain goes over a cliff in an automobile and crashes on the rocks below, who cares if the figure at the wheel is really a dummy? Who cares if the "blood" spurting out of the hero's chest actually comes from a ketchup capsule? Who cares if the heroine trudging through the "Sahara" is really a few feet from a Taco Bell on the edge of the Mojave Desert in California? Who cares?

The tedious, intricate process of moviemaking doesn't really matter as long as we are taken in by an illusion of a real world. If Tom Hanks, who was about ten years old when John F. Kennedy was assassinated, can shake hands with a filmed image of that president in *Forrest Gump* (1994), we know it's a trick but we enjoy it. So I wonder just what I *can* or *should* tell movie fans about the moviemaking process without spoiling the fun of moviegoing. And I conclude that it should be just about what I have told film students at Dartmouth College for more than thirty years. Some students took my courses because they wanted to make films (and a few succeeded), but the majority were simply fulfilling a distribution requirement in the humanities with an offbeat course in a subject they liked and thought they knew something about. Today, other students sign up for television-oriented media courses and revel in academic approaches to MTV or sitcoms like *Friends*.

Well, I have no argument with conferring academic respectability on popular subjects like the movies, comic strips, or television. I may, however, object to some of the academic jargon used to describe what everyone should recognize as commercial entertainment. But I would never have been allowed (much less paid) to teach a mundane film course at a respected Ivy League institution if an enlightened academic had not come up with the perfect answer (the history of film is in cans!) to the objection that film courses have no place in higher education.

So here, gleaned from a variety of courses that I have taught, is a simple primer for beginning film students or laypersons about the movies. It begins, as has every course I have taught, with a brief history and concludes with an apology for using older films to illustrate a point of view. The brief history does call attention to significant movies from the past and from abroad with which a true film buff should be acquainted. This is followed by a description of the moviemaking process, which is broken down into five essential steps—literary (nothing happens until a script is written), administrative (money raising and production planning), shooting, editing, and the very costly process of marketing. Because I was a magazine film critic for several years, there is a chapter on how critics work and how studios woo their favor. And because I intend this volume to be an all-inclusive report, there are chapters about the various forms that movies can and have taken: nonfiction as *actualité* or documentary in its various forms—as information, propaganda, education, or even as entertainment; the avant-garde (film as film with no purpose except self-expression), and, of course, animation.

Despite its title, this volume does not really include *all* you should know about the movies. But it's a start.

1

A Brief History
of the Movies

"Courses in film do not belong in a college curriculum because they are not backed by a significant body of literature." So said the chairman of Dartmouth's Committee on Instruction in 1964. What the chairman meant was that few if any textbooks were available. By contrast, film instructors today are swamped with books about the movies. No first-rate textbook publisher is without a hefty, illustrated tome purporting to be the "best," "most comprehensive" single volume of film history. Probably the most popular is David Cook's *History of Narrative Film* (1996), now in its third edition.

Despite having taught eight or nine different film courses and despite the fact that no self-respecting film studies program is without various courses in film history, I must confess that I have taught only one such course, a joint effort with my daughter a few summers ago to shed some light on Hollywood's so-called Golden Era—the thirties—a period that I experienced firsthand in Hollywood.

Courses in film history are not unimportant, but how much can anyone learn about movie output in ten, twenty or thirty weeks? Reading a good film history book and then devoting a few years to looking at all kinds of movies from every period and from every country that excelled in moviemaking will make one very knowledgeable about film history. This means, of course, joining college film societies, attending art theaters, and watching the classic-movie channels on cable TV. It means becoming familiar with the origins of the medium— with the *actualités* of the Lumières, with the fanciful works of Georges Méliès, with Edwin S. Porter's classic Western, *The Great Train Robbery* (1903), with some of the D. W. Griffith Biograph short subjects and then his *Birth of a Nation* (1915), *Intolerance* (1916), and *Broken Blossoms* (1919). It means looking at (and probably enjoying) the works of the great comedians—Chaplin, Keaton, Lloyd, and Langdon. It means managing to see at least part (the synchronous-sound part) of *The Jazz Singer* (1927) as well as the sound-oriented gangster films—*Little Caesar, The Public Enemy,* and *Scarface*—that dominated the early years of the 1930s and led to what we call the Golden Era featuring luminous stars like Garbo, Dietrich, Lombard, Muni, Gable, Grant, and Tracy, running the gamut from sentimental slop to screwball comedy.

It all began, of course, with the *actualité*—the documentary. For their nickels and fifty centimes early moviegoers got to see the world around them in motion on a screen. The first films by the Lumière brothers in France showed simple events from everyday life: workers leaving their factory; a train pulling into a station; fishermen setting out from the docks. Such events were very exciting to audiences in the mid-1890s. They became even more exciting when the Lumières sent their cameramen to far-off places to bring back moving pictures of locations the audience members would never visit in person.

As everyone knows, this marvelous invention, which continued to be used as a recording instrument to capture scenes and events from around the world, soon came to be used to record staged events as well. A girl in bloomers would climb a ladder while the camera shot this delectable sight from below. In the United States, Thomas Edison's cameras would show May Irwin kissing John Rice. And if incidents could be staged, why not stories? The Lumières' real-life reproductions in France were soon challenged by the imaginative fiction of Georges Méliès and subjects like his *Trip to the Moon* (1902). Stories could be told with the camera fixed as if viewing a stage. Stories could be told more effectively when one setup was joined with another through editing and when the camera was used to show the same scene from different angles or even with movement.

Thus came the birth of the fiction or "entertainment" movie, which was to capture the fascination of the entire world, a fascination that has lasted to this day and far exceeds the attraction of *actualités*. Whereas nonfiction has always dominated the publishing world (the Bible and Dale Carnegie's *How to Win Friends and Influence People* easily outsell *Gone with the Wind*), the nonfiction film or documentary is no more than a poor relative in movie distribution, its main outlet being in a TV ghetto or on the Public Broadcasting Service. Nevertheless, documentaries are still made everywhere in the world. They are usually films of serious intent, though some are humorous, made in remote parts of the world by people who have something to say and have acquired the skill (as well as a knack for raising money) that makes it possible to communicate with audiences through the movie medium. I emphasize "communicate" to differentiate these films from so-called independent films—regarded by some critics as works of art—which are made as personal statements without regard to audience comprehension. There was a time, however—in the twenties—when the nonfiction form was largely dominated by poets, artists, and the avant-garde, who used their skill with the camera to produce small films that were unique in style and form and had only the most oblique type of message.

Man Ray, an American photographer living in France, produced short films that exploited the human body; French artist Fernand Léger did a famous short subject, *Ballet Mécanique* (1924), which used cogs, cams, and gear to fill the screen with intriguing images but with no story at all. Then there was a spate of poetic "city" films, which said something about life in cities as diverse as New York, Paris, Berlin, and Moscow but were essentially visual exercises exploiting the potential of the camera to slow down or speed up action, distort reality with very wide lenses or prisms, and so on.

My good friend the late Ralph Steiner, a superb still photographer who was obsessed by water images throughout his life, made a short film entitled *H2O* (1929), which, among other things, examined a drop of water from various angles. Fifty years later he went to Northampton, Massachusetts, and did a ten-minute film concentrating on a pond, including drops of water, in a place called Look Park.

Although some artists were enjoying the potential of the moving picture medium, others were attempting to use the nonfiction movie form for profit, sometimes with great success. I think of the purveyors of newsreels, travelogues, and oddities, which had been staples of movie theater programming from the start. Indeed the capability of newsreel cameramen to photograph major events makes the archives of those who own the libraries of newsreel companies extremely valuable. But when people think of movies, they think of the stars, the production values, and the magic.

Looking back at the thirties, we are apt to recall the great works of 1939 that are still viewed with pleasure today—*Gone with the Wind, Stagecoach, The Wizard of Oz, Rebecca.* It is easy to forget the industry-wide retrenchment of World War II that had most leading men donning uniforms and much of the creative talent of writers, directors, editors, and cinematographers turned to the documentary, which could build morale and justify the sacrifices that people were being called on to make.

An abortive attempt by returning veterans to make postwar movies that supported FDR's four freedoms led to a highly publicized investigation of the industry by the House Un-American Activities Committee, a manifestation of the Cold War that resulted in an industry-wide blacklist of all employees (including me) who were accused of having Communist affiliations. This threat of thought control occurred just as antitrust laws forced the industry to divorce itself from theater ownership and the offer of free television in the home decimated the movie theater audience. (Some say the industry was actually lucky to get out of the theater business when theater attendance plummeted.)

Another significant postwar development was the renaissance of international film production and the growing awareness of its quality through the release of foreign films in the United States. It should be noted that movies were an international phenomenon from the start. Development of film, cameras, and projection girdled the earth during the last decade of the nineteenth century and the first decade of the twentieth. Although the principal sources of invention were in France (with the Lumières) and in the United States (with Edison), film production thrived in Germany, England, Scandinavia, Italy, and Japan.

It was, in fact, the Italian spectacles—four-reel efforts such as *Quo Vadis?* (1912)—that broke the U.S. pattern decreed by the Patents Trust under Edison of one reelers, or ten-minute films. D. W. Griffith's version of Alfred Tennyson's poem *Enoch Arden* (1911) required two reels, but the trust that controlled Biograph (under whose aegis the movie was made) insisted on running it in two ten-minute parts. This issue led to Griffith's leaving Biograph and ultimately making the four-reel *Judith of Bethulia* (1914) and the incredibly innovative and successful but politically incorrect three-hour epic, *Birth of a Nation* (1915).

The introduction of sound in the late 1920s temporarily put a halt to international film exchange. Dubbing films into various

languages didn't always work (try saying *auf wiedersehen* instead of *ta ta* and you'll get the idea), and moviegoers resisted
subtitles. The result was that foreign films were confined to a
few art houses in big cities. After World War II, however, there
was a strong renewal of domestic interest in films from abroad.
This began with the "discovery" of neorealism—grim but lifelike stories of ordinary people from an Italy recently liberated
from the iron heel of Mussolini's Fascism. The interest in for-
eign-language films was fanned by the sudden surge of cre-
ativity in France that we called the New Wave. Anyone seri-
ously interested in film history had to become familiar with the
work of new names in the directorial ranks such as Godard,
Truffaut, Richardson, Bergman, and Bertolucci but also had to
be familiar with at least some of the works of Luis Buñuel,
Michelangelo Antonioni, Carol Reed, David Lean, Satyajit Ray,
Luchino Visconti, Carl Th. Dreyer, Robert Bresson, and Akira
Kurasawa. And that imposing list of names does not include
the "big" names of American moviemaking, many of whom—
such as John Ford, William Wellman, Howard Hawks, Frank
Capra, George Stevens, and Raoul Walsh—had been part of the
moviemaking process since it moved to Hollywood. Others—
such as Stanley Kubrick, Orson Welles, Billy Wilder, William
Wyler, Ernst Lubitsch, Fritz Lang, and Alfred Hitchcock—received their training elsewhere but became giants of the American screen.

Having used directors as linchpins on which to peg a
moviegoer's approach to movie history, let me now reverse
myself completely and state that the actual history of the
movies consists more accurately in the never-ending search
for story material. Academics who exalt work in what they
choose to call (I think incorrectly) "the cinema" ignore the importance of content. The truth is that the production of movies
has always begun, and will always begin, with the search for
story material. In the very early days, when movies were short
and were turned out in quantity, it was customary to buy
story ideas wherever they could be found and to use the sub-

ject matter of well-known public-domain novels condensed to the popular ten-minute format. D. W. Griffith is said to have personally directed or produced 450 films between 1908 and 1912. The list of titles is staggering and includes Tolstoy's *Resurrection*, Shakespeare's *The Taming of the Shrew*, Tennyson's *Enoch Arden*, and *A Corner in Wheat* (based on Frank Norris's novel *The Pit*).

The demand for best-selling novels continues to this day, and for good reason. Not only do novels provide ready-made characters and story material, but they are, to a certain extent, presold. Hemingway's *For Whom the Bell Tolls* had been a Book of the Month Club selection and was probably read by a million people. But the movie version (1943) with Gary Cooper and Ingrid Bergman, though not a great hit, was probably seen by 25 million. On the other hand, a fairly obscure novel by James Herlihy, *Midnight Cowboy*, might have had a thousand readers but the movie version (1969), a big hit, was seen by more millions than the adaptation of Hemingway.

Moviemaking goes through five important and interrelated but distinct steps. The first is *literary*—a story must be found and a script written. The second is *administrative*—the script is used to raise money and serves as the basis for production planning. The third, *shooting*, and the fourth, *editing*, are self-explanatory. The fifth and final step is *distribution*—marketing, promoting, and selling, which, in this day of varied markets, represents about 50 percent of the budget and can, like the other four steps, effectively alter the finished product—the movie itself.

What follows is a fuller explanation of these steps.

2

✢

Getting Started

Making a movie is a complicated process whether it is a feature film for theatrical release, a short subject, a documentary, or a film produced for television. One can be a serious movie buff without knowing much about the nuts and bolts of the moviemaking process, but I never teach a film-related course without spending at least one session explaining the procedure.

I grew up in Hollywood, haunting the M-G-M back lot throughout my childhood and then working as a Hollywood screenwriter for about ten years. Nevertheless, I must confess that I had only the vaguest idea of how movies were made until I was given total responsibility for turning out rather modest independent sponsored films during the 1950s, when I was barred from employment in the entertainment-movie industry because a few people had fingered me as an alleged Communist.

It is also true that during the ten-year period when I wrote screenplays in Hollywood, the only time I had an opportunity to see what I had written recorded on film was for my first movie, *We Went to College* (1936). I was on the set of that movie only because, as a recent college graduate, I was used as a technical adviser.

Making movies is extremely compartmentalized. It doesn't take a computer expert to know what can be achieved with computerized special effects. One does have to know which computer experts should be hired.

As a writer, I like to emphasize that nothing happens until a script is written. Certainly, none of the other steps can proceed, whether it is a feature, an animated cartoon, or a documentary that is under consideration. The degree to which the proposed subject is described in full, say, as a screenplay with all the dialogue and action, depends on the medium and, to some extent, on the style of the likely director, though the written subject is frequently completed with no director in mind. A documentary presented as cinema verité, in which events and people are to be shot and recorded as they are rather than as staged, obviously cannot be written beforehand. But the objective can be outlined, and the locations and people to be photographed can be specified and usually are.

But a completed screenplay, an outline, or a proposal has no life of its own if no one agrees to finance its production. Thousands of original screenplays are written every year. Some are optioned or purchased. A handful are made. To progress from step one—the literary—to step two—the administrative—requires someone who is interested in the project on the basis of what is written and finding financial support, which often is possible only if a director or a star or both have shown equal interest. Then—and only then—does the project move to step two, in which what has been written becomes the blueprint for the production-planning process—kind of a battle plan to turn written pages into film.

The experts (called production managers) who work out these battle plans must have some idea of the available budget before they can break down a script for the most efficient procedure. Cost can be estimated on a maximum or a minimum basis, and it will be affected by the going price of the proposed director and stars. It is probably the production manager who will influence the decision as to whether the movie will be shot in the Sahara or in California's Mojave Desert. And when he lays out the shooting schedule, he will certainly see to it that an introductory scene in Grand Central Station is shot back-to-back with the climax, which takes place in the same location. He will also note that all the scenes that include Marlon Brando, who might be paid close to a million dollars a day, can be shot in two days if mattes are used to change the backgrounds from Manhattan to Southern California.

Production managers prepare flow charts—using the numbered scenes in shooting scripts—to indicate the most efficient use of locations, cast, crew, and equipment. Incidentally, the numbers in a script (which are added when the script is approved by the producer for shooting) are used not only by the production manager but also by the assistant cameramen to slate every shot, by the script supervisor to record what is in the shot, and by the editor to catalog what he receives from the lab.

Production managers and front-office moneymen have been known to profoundly affect not only the course of shooting but also the content of movies. It is said that halfway through the shooting of the adaptation of James Michener's *Hawaii* (1966) an order came down, based on cost, to cut an entire subplot out of the script. Who, then, is the true auteur of *Hawaii*? Is it Dalton Trumbo, whose 250-page script was emasculated? Is it director George Roy Hill, who followed orders? Or is it the cost-cutting zombie in the front office who cut forty pages out of the script to save money?

3

Story Material

When you view a movie and try to evaluate it, remember that the most difficult task in moviemaking is finding story material. Producers, who have dominated the movie industry since its inception, play the principal role in looking for suitable subject matter. Novels, plays, biographies, historic events, even well-publicized current happenings as reported in the press, have always been used as film sources. Of the films released in 1993, it is interesting to note how many were adaptations of novels, plays, and even works of nonfiction. *Six Degrees of Separation* was from a currently successful play and Shakespeare's *Much Ado about Nothing*, from a timeless one. *Schindler's List* and *In the Name of the Father* were derived from nonfiction books. *Shadowlands*, about Joy Gresham's relationship with British author C. S. Lewis, was clearly based on fact. *The Age of Innocence* and *The Remains of the Day* were based on novels. *Gettysburg* was, of course, based on Civil War history. Considering the present obsession with sex and violence, one would expect the Louise Woodward au pair murder trial and President Bill Clinton's affair with Monica Lewinsky to be turned into movies for theater screens or television, and they probably will be.

But there are and always have been originals—in 1993, *The Piano* and *In the Line of Fire,* among others. Some of the films I have liked best in the past few years—modest ones at that— were originals. *The Brothers McMullen* (1995) is an example. Some of the worst films of recent years have also been originals, including the sexually explicit *Basic Instinct* (1992), which was sold to Warner Bros. by Joe Eszterhas for $3 million, the highest price in history for an original screenplay. (The story cost went even higher when the producers felt compelled to bring in other writers for rewrites.)

Three million dollars is, however, a fair-size hop, skip, and jump from the fifteen dollars Anita Loos (later to become famous as the author of *Gentlemen Prefer Blondes*) got from D. W. Griffith in 1912 for her one-page story, "The New York Hat." Considering that moviemakers such as Griffith were turning out as many as fifty short movies a year—many of them one-reelers that ran ten minutes—it is not surprising that a market was created for original screenwriting. Fan magazines for readers in their teens and early twenties advertised home-correspondence courses in screenwriting that promised "fortunes to be made."

Since story material is still a principal concern of all moviemakers, I constantly emphasize to students eager to enter the industry that the most effective calling card to a potential employer is a screenplay with a unique story idea.

Selling a screenplay, however, is never easy. Thousands are written and submitted for each one that is sold. But *writing* movies is the one aspect of the production process that a newcomer can practice at home without any paraphernalia other than a pencil, a typewriter, or a word processor.

Most studios refuse to accept a screenplay unless it is submitted by a reputable agent. Most reputable and effective agents won't handle screenplays by unknown writers. If this sounds like a catch-22, it is. Despite the persistent hunger for new material, a story or screenplay—even one submitted by a "reputable agent"—is filtered through a rigid screening process before it gets any consideration at all.

In the thirties, a major studio like M-G-M employed thirty or forty professional readers. Since the search for story material was highly competitive, the reading of submitted material—screenplays, novels, short stories, or plays—was often duplicated from studio to studio. The comments of a reader regarding suitability could spell the difference between sale or no sale. One summer as a reader at M-G-M, I recommended the purchase of a *Saturday Evening Post* story called "Night Bus," by Samuel Hopkins Adams. M-G-M didn't buy it but Columbia did, and it became the source of their Academy Award winner, *It Happened One Night* (1934).

A reader's job is to provide the producers with a quick and efficient summary of literary material. They may decide whether the subject interests them on the basis of a three-line summary—"about a shipwreck and the romance between a sailor and an heiress when stranded on a desert island." If so, they read the one-page summary that follows. Then, if still interested, they read the detailed synopsis and the reader's comments. In rare instances, they might even read the source material itself. (It is said that David Selznick, producer of *Gone with the Wind* [1939], never did read the novel.) But that is how story material is found. Considering that Hollywood once turned out 500 movies a year, the story search process is critical to a studio's success. And the search often includes synopsizing literary classics (referred to as the public domain) that can be turned into movies without paying authors anything at all. Hence, *David Copperfield* (1935), *Romeo and Juliet* (1936), and *Tess* (1979).

Because of the importance of storytelling in movies, I usually begin a course for budding screenwriters by asking them
to write the story of a movie in treatment form. And because
stories are hard to make up, I usually give them a carefully
chosen published work (preferably one in the public domain)
to adapt for the screen in treatment form. (I say "carefully chosen" because I must believe that the novel, short story, or play
does indeed have potential as movie material.)

The question is usually asked, "But what is a treatment?"
The answer is that it is a general description of a movie in
prose. To write a treatment, write down the story of a movie
you have just seen in which you describe story content without necessarily specifying movie technique. (The assign-
ment is not too unrealistic. I suggest that any student seeking a job in Hollywood or New York might meet a potential
employer handing out a literary property in which he has an
interest and asking the job seeker to read it and return in a
few days with an outline of how the subject should be dealt
with as a movie.)

In my classes I tell students that they can use as much or as
little of the original material as they want, as long as the subject is not too well-known by the general public. On the other
hand, Orson Welles did a stage production of Shakespeare's
Julius Caesar using Fascist Italy rather than ancient Rome as its
setting. He also did a Haitian *Macbeth*. It is perfectly legitimate
to take liberties with source material. In some of my classes,
nineteenth-century novels have received modern settings,
with pirates becoming dope smugglers.

If the original structure can be followed, then it is the student's task to describe how the events and relationships can
be shown in movie terms. Students are urged to look for the
key sequences and to explain how they can be tied together.
Above all, they should try to find an interesting opening because the reader whose attention is not caught on the first
page will read no further. Thus, if anything is to be written
with specificity in movie style, it is the opening. Then, sur-

prisingly enough, the clearer the writer is about what she wants to tell, the more concise she can be.

By eliminating the need to make up characters or a basic story line, I give the students a chance to see what is unique about movie storytelling. They see at once that a prose writer has the luxury of describing his characters with words, whereas a movie writer must provide this description by what the characters say or do or by what others say about them— which is not always reliable.

Plays often begin with the servants or members of a family talking about a character who is soon to make an entrance. In the opening of *Casablanca* (1942)—based on an unproduced play called *Everybody Comes to Rick's*—there is a great deal of talk about Humphrey Bogart's Rick before we ever see him. It's known as "building up an entrance," but it also serves as a way of providing information with spoken words.

Since I have done a few adaptations in my day—*They Gave Him a Gun* (1937), *Song of the South* (1946), *So Dear to My Heart* (1949), *Jennie* (1939), and *Cinderella* (1950)—I feel justified in explaining some of my methods.

I usually do a step sheet as I read through the book, play, or novel to be adapted. Then I draw up a cast of characters. And then I try to write the essence of the subject in a paragraph. This is usually an attempt to find the primary conflict or the goal of the protagonist. If I can't do that based on what I have read, I know that I am going to have to invent something. In the case of *Cinderella,* for example, we know that she is a slave in her stepmother's house who will want to go to a ball at the palace. So my first draft began with an incident to present the news about the ball and establish Cinderella's desire to go and to set up the stepmother and the stepsisters as the obstacles to that goal.

Having mentioned obstacles that lead to conflict, I might as well confess that the need for conflict—in scenes, sequences, and in a story as a whole—is something I can never emphasize enough. Conflict provides the basis for both drama and comedy, and its presence or absence explains why some movies work and some don't.

Other essential elements to look for in assessing the screen potential of story material include unique characters, interesting visual possibilities, two or three "set pieces," and an original premise that leads to an exciting and satisfying climax.

Prose can offer vivid visual description, but visual description is not required in a prose work. If visuals are missing, the screenwriter must supply them. Often scenes that take place in commonplace locations must be transposed to backgrounds that offer some visual interest or excitement.

This leads to consideration of "set pieces," which, depending on the subject matter, take place in specific but interesting locales (an amusement park, Mount Rushmore, a roadside motel) or are built around situations (earthquakes, car chases, fires) in which a substantial development in the story can take place. If the literary source does not include such elements, the screenwriter invents them.

This first phase of writing for the screen is in some ways the most pleasurable because the writer at that point is the total moviemaker. The whole world is at his fingertips; the sky is the limit. In the initial writing stage the writer has complete control of the material—the writer is the director, actor, cinematographer, editor, and musician. The writer is, for the moment at least, the only author.

But very few screenwriters have the privilege of following up this individual process by participating in actual production. Unlike playwrights who, under their Dramatists Guild contract, are present during rehearsals and must approve all suggested changes in their scripts, the screenwriter is seldom on the set at all, unless he wangles an invitation to satisfy his curiosity. There are exceptions, of course. Some directors have close relationships with certain writers and get a feeling of security when a writer (not always the one responsible for the shooting script) is at his elbow during shooting to make on-the-spot changes in dialogue or action. One thinks of enduring writer–director collaborations such as John Ford and Dudley Nichols, Frank Capra and Robert Riskin, Billy Wilder with Charles Brackett and, later, I. A. L. Diamond.

4

✢

About Screenplays

A moviegoer who knows nothing about the movies except that he likes them should understand the contribution that the screenplay makes to the finished result. Like the novelist, the screenwriter, unless he is writing about well-known people or events, starts with an audience knowing nothing (except what the press agent has slipped into the media; after all, it's pretty hard to keep an audience in the dark about *Shakespeare in Love*). Both novels and films communicate by conveying information. After all, they are about people and what they do and think. The methods that are used to convey information in interesting ways distinguish the technique of the novelist from that of the screenwriter. Graphic description of people, locales, and action requires a lot of words in written work, and it can be presented with great skill and charm. On the screen, the "look" of a person, a place, the weather, the sounds heard, and the action that takes place can be conveyed

instantaneously. The screenwriter may have to write at some
length to describe what he has in mind, but his words will not
appear on the screen. They are simply the blueprint for what
is to be shown and heard, and they need not be written in a
way that diverts the reader (though in some cases they are).
But what does the screenwriter do to describe mood or character? What are the visual equivalents for words like *cruel,
haughty, cowardly, generous?*

In *Tol'able David* (1921), Ernest Torrence is quickly characterized as a mean bastard when he starts to crush a kitten with a
rock. But a screenwriter cannot get away with such time-worn
characterizations anymore. Who would think of establishing a
villain by having him steal pencils from a blind man? Today,
characterization requires cumulative action and dialogue. In
some films—like Westerns—characterization is accomplished
with costumes. (Villains usually wear black, for example.)
Often the personality of the actor provides a shortcut. (Was
John Wayne or Robert Redford ever a villain?) But this
method can be unreliable. Who knows whether Robert De
Niro is supposed to be a devil or an angel? The point is that
screenwriters, like novelists, may write brilliant passages of
description about their characters or locales, but such writing
is not required. The screenwriter is required to provide the images, the spoken words, the actions, or the sound cues that get
his intentions across.

There are some outstanding examples of movie information that is handled with audience interest and entertainment in mind. In the opening of *Midnight Cowboy* (1969)—
and under the titles—we see Jon Voight, as Joe Buck, getting
dressed in an outlandish deerskin suit, admiring himself in
a mirror, and striding across town in his western boots car-
rying a cowhide suitcase to the kitchen of a small café. Here
the dialogue reveals that although he is late for work at his
menial job, he doesn't care because he is quitting. A brief dialogue scene with a black dishwasher who is his friend reveals this alteration of the status quo (a frequent necessity in

the first five minutes of a movie) and establishes Voight's goal that will give the movie its momentum: He wants to go to New York to be a stud, as illustrated by the following excerpt from Waldo Salt's script:

DISHWASHER

What do you want to do back east?

JOE BUCK
There are a lotta rich women back there, Ralph. Beggin' for it. Payin' for it, too.

DISHWASHER
Yeah?

JOE BUCK
Hell yeah! And most of the men
are tutti-fruttis.

DISHWASHER
Must be some mess back there.

JOE BUCK
Well, I'm going to cash in on some of that. . . . !

We then follow Buck to New York and watch him face obstacles to his goal at every turn, a principal obstacle being his relationship with Rizzo the cripple (played by Dustin Hoffman), which ultimately leads to a new goal—taking care of the critically ill Rizzo—which brings about Buck's redemption.

The first three and a half minutes of *North by Northwest* (1959) introduce Cary Grant as an efficient, fast-talking advertising executive with disdain for his profession. He meets some clients in the Hotel Plaza bar, remembers that he must get a message to his mother, and signals to a bellhop who is paging a "Mr. Kaplan," which causes a pair of hoods to assume that Grant is Kaplan. When Grant follows the bellboy, they grab him, shove a gun in his ribs, and kidnap him.

Grant's status quo is certainly altered and a story is set in motion, even though a lot of information has been withheld. (Who are the hoods and why do they want Kaplan?) What we do know is that Cary Grant is on the spot and will try to escape, an immediate goal with the two hoods as obstacles. This illustrates a very useful piece of storytelling machinery: To have a character escape from something, have the character achieve something. Effective movie stories are all about motives, intentions, and goals. Intention is usually the cause of action, but its fulfillment is not guaranteed. There are always obstacles, complications, and counterintentions.

In Hitchcock films (e.g., *North by Northwest*), which are plots rather than narratives, the intentions are created by external circumstances. In the case of *North by Northwest*, it is only because Grant is mistaken for someone named Kaplan that a story is set in motion.

In a narrative, intentions and goals can be indigenous to the character. (Voight, in *Midnight Cowboy*, is a rural innocent who thinks his good looks will appeal to women and even to "tutti-fruttis" in New York, so that's where he goes to start the story.) Consider another example (and this one is made up): A girl comes to a big city to become a dancer. She goes to a tryout, is turned down, and is told that she needs more training. She can't afford dancing lessons, so she must earn some money to attend ballet school—a second objective. She gets a job as a waitress, but the owner of the restaurant wants to sleep with her and she wants to avoid him (another objective, etc.).

I am going through this basic material on story structure rather quickly, but I want to give some new grounds for evaluating movies. For the most part, individuals will continue to come away from movies with a "like" or "dislike" reaction. But as the noted French director Jean Renoir once said: "What you have to say is more important than the way you say it." I think it is useful to know why some stories seem to be told more effectively than others. The essence of good movie writing is to move a story forward in ways that make the audience eager to know what will happen next. The essence of a movie is that you see one action after another. The story is revealed in bits and pieces. We can endure trivia and banality as long as we have enough information to arouse our curiosity. And nothing involves us as much as watching a character in jeopardy, in conflict, or in pursuit of ostensibly unattainable goals.

Conflict is the great energizer. Without it—whether it's man against man, man against woman, man against the system, against a beast, against the elements, or, as is often the case in existential movies, man against himself—if there's no conflict, we are bored. This goes for movies as a whole and for scenes as well.

Take a key scene at the beginning of *Mr. Deeds Goes to Town* (1936), written by Robert Riskin and directed by Frank Capra (the first of his successful films about the common man versus the establishment, which came to be known as "Capracorn").

A rich man has died in a car crash, leaving his fortune to a Mr. Deeds (Gary Cooper), who lives in Vermont. Three shifty characters from a big-city law firm look for Deeds to give him the $20 million and also to see to it that he spends it in ways that profit them. When they get off the train in a small town in Vermont and ask for Deeds, they run up against a closemouthed Yankee stationmaster whose vocabulary is limited to "yup" and "nope." They are eager and he is reluctant. They need information but the guy who can provide it couldn't care less.

The lesson is that in making film stories work, in making individual scenes interesting, the shortest distance between two points is not always best. That's why most screenplays are never finished until, for whatever reason, someone in authority says, "Let's shoot it." With every line, every scene, every sequence, it always seems possible that there's a better way to get from here to there. And it is up to the writer to look for it.

Riskin could have made an abrupt cut from the decision in the crooked lawyers' office to look up Mr. Deeds to the same group ringing the bell at the front door of Deeds's Vermont house. But the two-minute scene with the reluctant station-master is more entertaining than a straight cut to the exterior of Deeds's house, and it provides some useful information about the contrast between staunch New Englanders and shifty city slickers, a foreshadowing of the lawyers' later relations with Deeds himself.

If you analyze films carefully, you'll see how often the proposed course of action is laid out early on. It's like a game in a way. You don't know the outcome, but some sort of rules and objectives are laid down—subject to change, to be sure—but with a direction. The action of *Mr. Deeds*, for example, begins with a car crash and a newspaper headline about the sudden death of a well-known millionaire. Then it goes to a newspaper office where the editor announces his goal: to find out what kind of person inherited the millionaire's money. Then we meet the millionaire's lawyers, who are in possession of the will and want to milk it for all it's worth. They want to keep the press out of it. That's the secondary goal, which conflicts with the editor's goal. The lawyers hire a raspy-voiced public relations man to help keep the story of Deeds as low-key as possible. The lawyers go to see Deeds and find that they have a queer duck on their hands. Complications arise when the newspaper editor sends a girl reporter to break the shield that the lawyers have built around Deeds.

Every heist movie is laid out according to similar rules. We hear what each character is supposed to do. Some of the group have their doubts. Who said it would be easy? But the game plan is worked out, and we watch it unfold with all its difficulties.

In *The African Queen* (1951), written by James Agee and directed by John Huston, there is a prologue in which Katharine Hepburn's missionary brother (Robert Morley) is killed and she is thrown together with an uncouth river captain

(Humphrey Bogart) in an effort to escape the advancing Germans. This represents a very marked alteration of the status quo and introduces another useful element of narrative energy—*strongly contrasting characters,* in this case, the prim sister of a missionary (Hepburn) and an uncouth, hard-drinking riverboat captain (Bogart). They find safety on Bogart's boat (the *African Queen*), but the plot machinery has run out of gas: time to introduce a new goal. Hepburn provides it, although it takes about four minutes of screen time to develop. They will go downstream, past a German fort and through treacherous rapids, until they come to a lake where there is a powerful German gunboat. Converting some oxygen tanks (which happen to be aboard the *African Queen*) into torpedoes, they will ram the gunboat (the *Louisa*) and sink it. As Hepburn outlines what they are to do, more or less providing the schemata for the rest of the movie, Bogart agrees that what she proposes would be effective, but he also points out that it is impossible to achieve: *goal versus obstacle.* But when Hepburn accuses Bogart of being unpatriotic, he grudgingly gives in. Then they act out what has been outlined. With faith and with the one element that had not been predicted—they fall in love—the plan succeeds.

The layout scene is told from multiple points of view. Hepburn does most of the talking and Bogart listens and reacts. (Reaction shots always give us the essential viewpoint of the listener.) The camera observes, but is it truly objective? After all, our viewpoint shifts from that of one character to another. The writer of the film—as well as the director and the editor—can easily dictate our viewpoint. A novelist can do this, too, except when he is limited by writing in the first person. Most critics think of this aspect of movie technique as the work of the director, and it can be. But more often than not it originates in the storytelling process and the writer is responsible. He may use the simple expedient of dialogue, to be sure, but he can also rely on detail, calling for observation of specific items that would not be noticed with the camera taking in a full shot.

The basic ingredient of movies is unquestionably the shot. Some people compare the shot to a word in prose. But it is more like a sentence: "Here is a gun." Certainly writers of prose can also particularize; their words and sentences are carefully ordered to describe action and to manipulate our sensibilities.

In Kate Chopin's novel *The Awakening* (1899), for example, we find this description (in chapter 27) of the heroine's mood after leaving her husband and renting a house of her own:

> She turned back into the room and began to walk to and fro down its whole length, without stopping, without resting. She carried in her hands a thin handkerchief which she tore into ribbons, rolled into a ball and flung from her. Once she stopped, and taking off her wedding ring, flung it upon the carpet. When she saw it lying there, she stamped her heel upon it, striving to crush it . . . (then to skip a little.). In a sweeping passion she seized a glass vase from the table and flung it upon the tiles of the hearth.

This is visual storytelling, movie style.

There is an excellent scene about the visual imagination in F. Scott Fitzgerald's unfinished Hollywood novel, *The Last Tycoon.* Fitzgerald himself was not very successful as a movie writer, but he wrote this scene to illustrate what makes movie storytelling unique. The Fitzgerald scene was used in the movie adaptation of *The Last Tycoon* (1976), written by Harold Pinter and directed by Elia Kazan with Robert De Niro playing Monroe Stahr, an Irving Thalberg–type producer, and Donald Pleasence as a noted British playwright who has written eighteen pages of dialogue to get across a story point. The producer (De Niro) tries to tell the British playwright that movies need visual action as well as words. The playwright (Pleasence) defends his work. He says his characters are dueling while they talk. Then the producer acts out a scene about a stenographer who enters the office and empties the contents of her purse on the desk. There are two dimes and a nickel; she puts the dimes back in her purse and leaves the nickel.

Then she crosses the room and burns her black gloves in a stove. The phone rings, and she answers and says, "I have never owned a pair of black gloves in my life."

When Stahr, the producer, ends his scene at this point, the playwright wants to know what happens next. The producer shrugs and says he is just making movies. "Then what was the nickel for?" the playwright asks.

Initially the producer says, "I don't know." But then he laughs and adds, "Oh, yes, the nickel was for the movies."

The playwright shakes his head and concludes that he will never understand the damn stuff, but the producer tells him, "Yes, you will, or you wouldn't have asked about the nickel."

Stahr was showing how you can tell story and arouse interest with the camera through a series of shots and a minimum of dialogue. There are many examples of this kind of storytelling in movies. The camera is used as a kind of paintbrush or pointer revealing information, and it is sometimes information that the characters themselves are unaware of. If the writer provides some information in a scene that arouses our curiosity, we will follow with interest what happens next. If, for example, a man puts a gun in his pocket and then walks down Main Street, looking this way and that, and enters a bank where there is a guard, we are sure to be interested— even if the gun-toting man is derailed by a chance meeting and nothing happens. This is sometimes described as the "loaded-gun" device. Alfred Hitchcock, in a book of interviews with François Truffaut, explains that interest can be aroused in a conversation between two characters talking about something as banal as the weather if the audience knows there is a third character outside the door, cocking a loaded revolver.

The more the writer knows about his characters, the easier it is for him to write scenes. One handbook on writing gives a shortcut to characterization using a series of captions beginning with the letter *p*: profession, personal life, point of view, and personality.

Any one of these—or all of them—may determine the thrust of the story that is told. If the character is a detective, a doctor, a dancer, or a taxi driver, the chances are his profession will have something to do with the story's milieu. It is hard to imagine that a character's profession would have no bearing on the events or relationships to be shown. Whether the profession is used or not, the writer himself should know what it is, just as he must know something about each character's personal life—rich, poor, married, divorced, living with a girlfriend or boyfriend—whether or not the information is a factor on screen.

We may never see a character alone on the screen, but the screenwriter should know what that character is like in the privacy of his or her bedroom or bathroom. It is safe to assume that the writer knows his characters very well, or should. He or she has probably written biographies of all the principal characters, including details that will be revealed only when needed, as well as details that may never be revealed at all.

Some of this information may be part of what is called the back story. Sometimes the back story is so important to the present action that it must be shown as well as talked about, as in *Casablanca* (1942). When we first meet Rick (Humphrey Bogart) as the owner of his cafe, he is something of an enigma. We observe his actions and hear him say, "I stick my neck out for nobody," but how do we find out about his background? For one thing, the local prefect, Renault (Claude Raines), brings up the fact—telling the audience at the same time— that Rick fought for the Spanish Loyalists. The Nazi Colonel Strasser, who has seen a file on Rick, gives us more information. Then, after wondering about his attitude toward Ilsa (Ingrid Bergman), we get that information too by means of a flashback to Paris when they met, romanced, and separated as the Germans advanced on the city. As a result of what we learn about Rick's relationship with Ilsa in Paris many years ago, we have enough information to become involved and concerned about what he will do when he faces the final dramatic choice—to let her leave Casablanca with her new husband or to keep her there for himself. These are the essentials of good storytelling—making the audience wonder and care about what will happen next.

Screenwriters—like most storytellers since Aristotle laid down the rules in his *Poetics*—know that conflict is the sine qua non of effective storytelling. Writers create interest by bringing together people who are opposites or have opposing viewpoints and by separating those who would normally be attracted to one another. Often the relationship between leading characters in a story has a built-in conflict that can lead to problems. Romeo and Juliet may fall in love at first sight, but we know the Montague–Capulet feud is sure to louse up their romance.

Two people in love can be terribly uninteresting unless we know (even if they don't) what obstacles stand in the way of their continued happiness. In *Cavalcade* (1933), a famous old movie written by Noël Coward, two lovers discuss their rosy future as they stand arm in arm, looking out to sea from the railing of a ship. When they walk away, the camera holds and then moves in on a previously concealed life preserver. On it is stamped "SS TITANIC." That scene takes a minute, as compared to the blockbuster love affair aboard the more recent *Titanic* (1997), which took more than three hours to unfold, illustrating how a savvy movie writer (adapting a scene from a Noël Coward hit play) can use the camera to reveal information.

In a scene near the climax of *The African Queen*, Bogart and Hepburn have successfully overcome most of the anticipated obstacles of their river journey, successfully passing the armed German fort and surviving the treacherous rapids, but finally running aground in a swamp. Bogart goes overboard and tries to drag the boat but makes no progress and is covered with leeches. Sick and defeated, he collapses on the deck in Hepburn's arms. She recites a prayer of thanks for their brief life together as they prepare to die, having failed in their goal to reach the lake where they intended to destroy the German gunboat. The camera pulls back from this tableau of defeat and pans away to reveal that the little steamer is less than fifty feet from its destination—the lake. The camera points toward the sky and we see storm clouds, then the beginning of a downpour. The water rises in every stream and in the swamp. The boat floats into the lake, Bogart stirs, and, in a moment of triumph that he shares with Hepburn, realizes they have reached their goal.

In the simplest sense, then, interesting movie characters have goals—either *positive* in the sense of wanting to achieve something like sinking the *Louisa* or *negative* in the sense of not wanting something like getting killed by a hit man. And the odd thing is that once a goal is achieved, it has to be replaced by another or the story is over. If the character who has been running away from a posse finally eludes his pursuers, there may be a moment of triumph and relief, but then a new problem must be introduced: The character has hidden in a shack, but when he looks around he finds himself surrounded by odious green men with two heads.

Even in rather structureless stories—*M*A*S*H* (1970), for example—separate goals are used to give each sequence a structure. Take the trip that Trapper and Hawkeye make to Tokyo. In this case, one innocuous goal—to play a round of golf—leads to another, more serious one—to save a child's life on the operating table. And you could name more of the same in that film—convincing the dentist he's potent, winning bets on the football game, exposing Hot Lips' affair with Frank Burns, and trying to find out whether Hot Lips is blond or brunet, which leads to showing her naked in the shower.

Plot premises are a little different, but they certainly lead to goals on the part of the characters involved. Some people like to refer to plot premises as what-if's or gimmicks.

One thing I pass on to the talented young people who take my class in writing for the screen is a brief handout of familiar plots and premises (at least as many as I can think of). Here it is:

Success story: Horatio Alger, David and Goliath, Jack and the beanstalk, Cinderella.

Prodigal son: a person leaves family, home, or sweetheart and establishes values to live an easier and more exciting life, usually with ruinous results so that he or she returns much chastened.

Sacrifice plot: whether of father, mother, brother, husband, sweetheart, or friend. Done these days with an ironic touch in which the sacrifice proves to have been in vain—as in *Mildred Pierce* (1945). *Stella* (1989) is a classic example of unrecognized mother love.

Love plot: not necessarily between the sexes, which is usually outlined by boy meets girl, boy loses girl, boy gets girl. Can be mother or father for child, brothers, friends, and so forth.

The triangle: most familiar way to work the love plot, involving two men and a woman or two women and a man or combinations thereof. As in *The Age of Innocence* (1993).

Domestic relations: problems of married life—parents and alienated children. *Kramer vs. Kramer* (1979), *Terms of Endearment* (1983).

Reformation of character: the hard guy who turns soft, the weakling who becomes tough, the crook who goes straight, the whore who performs a noble deed, etc., as well as the opposite.

Adventure plot: usually involves a quest—rescuing someone in distress or recovering something of value, like the Holy Grail or the Stepford files or the crown jewels. Can also be about achieving some seemingly unattainable goal, such as reaching the North Pole or canoeing down the Colorado River.

Heist plot: variation of the adventure plot in which the objective is to pull off a major theft or scam.

Detection plot: solving a crime.

Ideological conflict plot: putting together two people with sharply divided views, for example, on politics, sex, or religion. Like the relationship between the protagonists in *Mississippi Burning* (1988). Buddy cops, one who wants to kill the rascals and the other who wants to reform them.

Revenge plots: based on settling a score, righting some wrong, a family feud. From *Hamlet* to *High Noon* (1952).

Fantasy plots: here you have a number of plot possibilities—deals made with characters from heaven or hell, talismans or potions that give people unique powers—to fly, to become invisible, to predict the future, to live again. You name it.

Escape plots: most prison flicks, *La Grande Illusion* (1937), *Stalag 17* (1953), and so forth.

Grand Hotel plots: group of people with various problems in a given locale. Often begins or ends with a disaster affecting all, for example, a plane crash, an earthquake, or a fire.

Sci-fi plots: usually involving a desperate attempt by protagonists to combat threatening forces with superhuman powers that are usually extraterrestrial.

Mistaken identity plots: can be used for either comedy or drama or both. *North by Northwest* (1959) is an example.

Stranger in the house plots: used for comedy as in *The Man Who Came to Dinner* (1942) or for drama as in *The Lodger* (1944).

Road plots: someone has to or wants to go someplace and meets a variety of problems along the way, which may or may not alter the original goal.

What everyone should realize is that no matter how familiar the plot or premise, the important thing is how it is treated. How much freshness of character or background—or even topicality—that can be brought to it. Implicit in most plots is a goal of some kind for the principal character or characters—something wanted or something to be avoided—and an opposing force—whether a person, an institution, or a natural phenomenon interfering with the objective. And in a lot of movies, the objectives shift as the story progresses.

5

✢

About Shooting the Movie

The third step in the moviemaking process is shooting, or production, the aspect of moviemaking most familiar to moviegoers, not only because it has been frequently shown in movies about movies, but also because it involves actors and directors, the people most publicized in the movie world. The host of names that follows the end of a movie nowadays gives some indication of the hundred or more people involved in the production. I don't intend to describe them all, but bear in mind that the principals I describe all have a corps of assistants—often described by the mysterious title "best boy," which refers to an aide or apprentice to a specialist.

The director has one or more assistants who handle paperwork, make sure new locations are ready, give out calls to the cast, handle large crowds of extras in mob scenes, and so forth.

The *cinematographer* is said to paint with light. He supervises the lighting, determines the exposure setting, and sometimes establishes the appropriate camera moves to satisfy the director's intentions. He does *not* operate the camera, and some cinematographers are known to leave the set while an *operator*, or chief assistant, many of whom are first-line cinematographers themselves, actually shoots the scene. The first or second assistant loads magazines with film, threads film from magazines into the camera, and makes and holds up the slate, reciting its content for the sound track. A given scene has a number in the script, but when it is shot from various angles, each angle bears the script number plus letters from A to Z for the various angles and a "take" number from 1 to infinity. The assistant cameramen also record the slate information on each film magazine, together with a footage count for each take.

The *camera crew,* and especially the head cinematographer, works closely with the *gaffer* (the head electrician), who in turn gives orders to his assistants to place the lights and their accessories—screens, scrims, barn doors, and gobos (masking devices cut to produce the effects of outdoor shrubbery, venetian blinds, etc.).

The chief *sound engineer* also has several assistants who place microphones, lay cables, and keep written logs. The head sound person usually is responsible for mixing the elements recorded, sometimes from several microphone sources. In any given location, he will ask for two minutes of silence from cast and crew before "striking" in order to record a sound we are not even aware of that is known as "room tone." Listen to so-called silence anywhere, and you will hear it. In cutting from one dialogue take to another—even if it is of the same person—the use of continuous room tone makes the edited link acceptable.

The person who keeps a record of all this photography and sound recording is the *script supervisor,* a man or woman whose job is to write an explicit description of all the camera angles, the action filmed, and the actual words spoken (regardless of what is written in the script), as well as of every pertinent detail of the appearance of an actor or the setting.

This means keeping track of the direction of performers' movements, the condition of their hair, lengths of cigarettes, amount of liquid in glasses, and the like. Since a crew might work on the same set for several days to record what happens in a few minutes, it is apparent that the setting and the actors' appearance should remain precisely the same throughout. (Polaroid pictures can be very helpful in assuring uniformity, as can videotape, often used as a supplement to filming.) It is also the supervisor's job to remind the director if ad-libs depart from the dialogue in the script, as well as to act as a prompter-reminder when an actor forgets his lines. Then what the supervisor records—usually by transcribing notes at night—is sent to the film editor and becomes his primary link with shooting.

There are many other specialists who are always present—the *grip* (who handles camera accessories like tripods, platforms, cranes, and dollies and handles dolly moves when required), a *prop man* or two (the magicians of the crew who usually come equipped with trunks that can deliver any small item that is needed, from a whiskey glass to a heroin needle), wardrobe mistresses and masters, hairdressers, makeup specialists, a still photographer (at least one), transportation people (a certain number of Teamsters Union members are required, whether needed or not), carpenters, painters, and set dressers.

Then there are those who have worked on the project but whose actual presence may or may not be required: the set designer, the casting director, location scouts, publicity people, animal trainers, personal maids and valets for the performers, caterers, and assorted hangers-on.

So what is the specific procedure? How is a movie shot? First, there may be a general reading to overcome a chronic problem—actors don't always know what a movie is about, having read only their own lines. Sometimes this is followed by several weeks of rehearsal, using floor space without appropriate furnishings. Such rehearsals would ordinarily be confined to the principals signed to "length of the picture" contracts. More often than not, shooting begins according to the production flow chart, which is apt to call for exteriors to be shot first. Weather has always been a problem in moviemaking. Although both sunlight and rain can be created artificially, a rainy or foggy day may make outdoor shooting impossible and send a film crew indoors. For every day of scheduled exteriors, there is therefore a ready "cover set" that can be used in case of bad weather.

The average length of movie time for a page of script is one minute, and the number of pages covered in a day averages out to about three or four for dialogue scenes and unknown lengths for pages of description. (A chase, for example, might take a week to shoot even though it is described in a sentence.)

A director's personal style will also have a very specific effect on shooting time. (Nunnally Johnson, a writer and producer, once defined a director's role as seeing to it that actors didn't go home before five o'clock.) For the most part, every scene—no matter how short—is covered from a variety of camera angles. So, even if there is only one take for each angle (and that is seldom the case), the "coverage" of a scene (which makes it possible for the editor to alter it or to speed up or slow down the result) can take a lot of time. And if the director chooses a so-called long take, moving the camera so that no cuts are necessary, the actors need a lot of rehearsal and shooting may require more takes than if it had been broken up. Orson Welles, for example, favored long takes and used a rising crane to follow two characters up a flight of stairs in *The Magnificent Ambersons* (1942). But in the same film, when he had the family seated around a dinner table—where camera movement would be difficult—he used an establishing shot of the entire table from behind Dolores Costello, who sat at the head of the table, and shot the rest of the acrimonious discussion in *close-ups* and *two-shots*.

Any close-up of an individual or two-shot of characters can be made without showing the offscreen characters with whom they are interacting. But the looks back and forth must be consistent (and seldom directly into the camera), as if the camera were always on one side, not on alternating sides of the people observed. It is worth noting how alternating "over the shoulder" close-ups of two people facing each other is accomplished. The camera may seem to switch from one person's viewpoint to the other's, but it views both from a single side which is, in effect, from the audience's viewpoint. And that is the essence of the director's objective in any scene: to provide his editor with material that enables him to take the eye of the viewer (in effect, the camera) precisely where it wants to go. The camera can, of course, go where the human eye cannot. So movies provide a view of action that is much more versatile and informative than what one can see through a window or from an orchestra seat in a theater. (Consider the current prevalence of overhead shots, for example.)

There are other factors to be considered for every shot. Of primary importance is *light*. What is its source—a window, a table lamp, an overhead chandelier? Once established in a shot, it must be maintained. Consider its *intensity:* is the light bright or dim? Does it fall on one character and leave another in shadow? And bear in mind that consistency demands that there be a change in the placement of offscreen lights for every setup.

The sun is the best source of light available, but it moves inexorably during the course of a day. So how do we control it? By using reflectors and by overriding it with electric lights that simulate daylight. This can be achieved with blue dichroic filters.

Anyone who has done still photography knows that you get vastly different effects with short versus long lenses, wide-angles versus telephotos. Movie directors and cinematographers use wide-angle lenses to provide maximum depth of field when they want subjects to stay in focus from the back of the screen to the front (a bottle of poison on a table in the foreground, the victim approaching it from the rear). An extremely wide-angle lens known as a fish-eye will distort the picture completely; a head close-up with this lens will show a much enlarged nose. A telephoto lens, on the other hand, will bring a background unnaturally close to a foreground character or object and will focus sharply on only one plane of the picture. If a subject runs toward a camera equipped with a 1,000 millimeter lens—as Dustin Hoffman does when he rushes to the church at the end of *The Graduate* (1967)—he seems to be going nowhere.

A 35 millimeter camera blimped to shut out the sound of its motor is a big and clumsy instrument. It is usually mounted on a precision-tooled small vehicle called a "crab dolly" with a seat behind it for the operator, who can raise the camera, lower it, and pan. Since the back wheels turn easily, it can be moved effectively by the grip. On a smooth surface, it can move in any direction. It can move in front of actors or follow them. It can move alongside. A sense of movement can also be achieved by attaching a zoom lens to the camera. Zooming, which can convert a single lens from wide-angle to telephoto or vice versa, can move the camera eye close to objects that it could never reach otherwise—a window in a skyscraper, for example. Or it can make it possible to go from a close shot of a person or an object to a long shot without a cut. But the effect is different from that achieved if you actually move the camera itself. Sometimes the focus is switched in a given location from a foreground person or object to one in the background or vice versa. This is known as using "rack focus."

Camera angles and movements are not usually prescribed in modern shooting scripts. The action is described in what is called a "master scene," and the angles or movements are left to the discretion of the director and cinematographer. But if camera directions are needed for storytelling purposes, the writer supplies them. In *Casablanca* (1942), for example, the script calls for an INSERT OF A MAN'S HAND writing "O.K. Rick" before we PULL BACK TO REVEAL Rick (Humphrey Bogart). Writers are apt to be quite specific in describing how transitions are to be handled with sound or picture or both.

The following extract from Buck Henry's screenplay for *The Graduate* (1967) indicates time passage in the hero's clandestine relationship with the wife of his father's law partner, Mrs. Robinson (played by Anne Bancroft).

EXT. BRADDOCK BACKYARD AND POOL AREA—DAY

We see Mrs. Braddock (Ben's mother) in the kitchen. Ben (Dustin Hoffman in the movie) comes through the back door, moves to the pool and dives in. The raft floats in the center of the pool.

SHOT—UNDERWATER

Ben swims toward us the length of the pool.

SHOT—AT THE WATERLINE

Ben surfaces and, in one movement, pulls himself up on the raft and—

INT. TAFT HOTEL ROOM—NIGHT

—lands on top of Mrs. Robinson on the bed. He stays on top of her for a moment.

—MR. BRADDOCK'S (Ben's dad) VOICE
—Ben—what are you doing?

Ben turns toward us and looks.

EXT. BRADDOCK BACKYARD AND POOL AREA—DAY
SHOT—POV OF BEN ON RAFT

Mr. Braddock standing by the side of the pool. The sun is behind him.

—BEN'S VOICE
Well, I would say that I'm just drifting.

If the ingredients for a transition are called for in a screen-play, it is up to the script supervisor to remind the director to adhere to the script and to provide the necessary visual or audio material. Mechanical transitions such as simple cuts, fades, dissolves, wipes, and an occasional iris (which involves a circle reduced in size until it leads to a complete fade-out) are devised in the important fourth stage—editing—and accomplished when the movie is printed in the lab.

6

+

Editing and Postproduction

Anyone familiar with moviemaking will tell you that a movie is actually made three times—by the writer, by the director, and by the editor. And it is the editor who gets the last crack at it. The editor's job usually begins with a review of the "rushes" (or "dailies") with the director and producer. Although every "take" is not printed, there may be several for each camera angle. The director or producer will choose the "best" take and may go so far as to tell the editor in what order to use the takes. "Start with the establishing shot to bring them to the table, go to the medium shot of Bogart and Bacall where he winks at her, then a close shot of the old guy watching them, then back to the medium shot, followed by alternating over the shoulder shots of B and B." Or the director may just tell the editor to use his judgment to assemble a "rough cut," including all the action and dialogue in the script. A rough cut, which can be assembled as the film is shot, may run an hour or more longer than the desired length of the finished product, even though the editor trims each take to its essentials.

At this point the fine-tuning comes in. As a rule of thumb, the editing process is expected to take about twice as much time as the shooting. Bear in mind also that until recently, a director had no rights at all in the editing process unless he had the clout to demand it in his original contract. Under the new contract negotiated by the Directors Guild a few years ago, the director now has the right to supervise—and to be paid for—a "first cut." But the editor starts to put a movie together as he gets the first "prints" of the dailies from the lab.

In this fourth stage—the editing process—there are infinite possibilities for manipulation because picture and sound are on separate rolls of film. Although the editor follows the script and the notes on shooting provided by the script supervisor, he can alter the continuity, cut out dialogue, and add new sounds (effects or even dialogue). He can (and usually does) speed up or slow down the tempo. And since he (or she) is the one who prepares the instructions to the lab for printing, he can even create special visual effects—freeze frames, slow motion, superimposed titles, rain or fog, earthquake shaking, and so forth. (I am describing the traditional methods of film editing. Today, film and synchronized sound are often transferred to tape and edited electronically—digitally. Altering images, speeds, backgrounds, and foregrounds can be done effectively, if not easily.)

There are basically three kinds of sound transitions that may or may not appear in the screenplay. They are frequently devised by the editor, who prepares all transitions in any case. (1) Dialogue, sound effects, or music of an outgoing scene carry over to the beginning of the incoming scene. (2) Sounds of the incoming scene are heard over the end of the outgoing scene. (3) A loud, sharp sound (e.g., a bell, a scream, a gunshot, the roar of a speeding car, or a blast of music) is used for its shock effect in introducing a new scene. Another kind of transition used to compress time and story development is generally put together out of many short shots by people known as montage experts. The impact of an entire war can be shown in a few seconds, beginning with a newspaper head-line, marching troops, cannons being fired, a cemetery with white crosses, another headline, "Armistice," and so forth. A girl can go from the farm to the big city and rise from secre-tary to executive with carefully selected shots and captions. The screenplay can specify the types of shots required or may simply call for a "montage of Sally's success in the Big Apple."

Reaction shots and cutaways are essential to trimming the length of a film. For example, you can't cut out a section of an actor's dialogue while the camera is on him or her. But if you can cut away to the listener or to a clock on the wall, you hear the actor continuing in voice-over but you can chop out a big chunk of speech and go back to the actor still talking in the same take or in a different one. Comparing any shooting script with the transcript of the final film will reveal how often this is done.

The other critical benefit of having sound and picture sep-arate occurs when the editor prepares the elements for what is called "the mix"—the final stage of production. At this point, the edited visuals can be projected from single reels (though without laboratory effects), but there may be as many coordinated sound reels as needed to provide a bal-anced sound sandwich—key elements being speech, effects, and music. But each of these categories may consist of many parts. Birds may be heard chirping over the roar of water over rocks with the motor noise of a car on a highway that is also visible in the scene. Music may be heard on the car radio or may be used to create a background mood. And be-cause the level of all these sounds must be adjusted to a point that seems realistic to the ear of someone in the audi-ence, a mixer at a console consisting of many volume con-trols must constantly adjust the sound level of each incom-ing sound track. Since big-budget feature movies have been known to mix more than twenty separate sound tracks, it stands to reason that mixing must be handled in stages. The first task may be to mix the dialogue, which can require three or four tracks on its own. Why? Because scenes in the same location are recorded at different times and thus the recording levels vary, as does the background noise (remember room tone). But consistent levels must be maintained in the final film. So dialogue is broken up into A and B and sometimes C rolls. Bogart starts his speech on A. The second part of his speech, which comes from another take, will be used as voice-over and will come in on roll B. The end of the speech is back to A, but the slight overlap of an interruption by Bacall is on C. A mixer who has two hands can balance three "pots," as they are called, but if he had to handle music and sound effects at the same time, he would lose control. So he separates mixes of the three key elements (dialogue, music, and effects) and then does another mix of those remaining. The result is the sound "sandwich" you hear in the theater.

The mixed sound track is usually sent to the laboratory on high-quality quarter-inch magnetic tape and transferred to a negative optical track on one edge of a strip of 35 or 16 millimeter film so that a composite print of picture and sound can be run off in large quantities for distribution.

The modern film lab is capable of considerable magic on its own and the editor, often with the direct help of the cinematographer, can request a number of miracles to improve the quality of the picture, not the least of which is the proper light balance of every scene and between one shot and another. This is executed by a "timer" who can brighten scenes that are underexposed and darken those that are overexposed. The lab (or related special-effects companies) also handles the superimposition of titles at beginning and end, as well as the use of split screens, freezes, and blowups.

Editor Ralph Rosenblum, now deceased, told a story about a burlesque performance scene in *The Night They Raided Min-*

sky's (1968) that required a lot of cutaways to the audience because there was limited footage of one of the performers, Bert Lahr, who had died during the shooting. Unfortunately, the director had provided only two full shots of the audience, and Ralph knew that cutting to the same two shots over and over again would look ridiculous. He solved the problem by having blowups made to provide him with a half dozen close-ups of people in that audience. A lab miracle!

This brief description of moviemaking is not intended to spoil the fun of watching movies, but if you are a frequent moviegoer, you should know how the picture you see on the screen is put together. And when you look at movies—especially if you see a movie more than once—you should try to figure out how some of the magic is accomplished. Notice the difference between "real" time and "film" time (which could be called "reel" time), and the difference between long takes and short takes. Bear in mind that long takes have to be real time, whereas short takes can give the impression of real time but can also alter time. Pay special attention to the way one scene leads to another. Notice how colors and shapes are matched or contrasted. Effective transitions are a major responsibility of the screenwriter in giving momentum to storytelling technique. Screen transitions are totally different from and infinitely more versatile than the methods available to the playwright or novelist.

One other bit of movie magic—the basis of almost all special effects—is the "matte shot." When an actor, actress, or object is shot against a blue background, a silhouette matte of the person or object can be superimposed on a background of choice—two people at a table on a balcony overlooking the harbor of Rio de Janeiro, for example, or the driver of a car on a treacherous mountain road. You shoot the characters or objects in the studio and superimpose the result on a background obtained halfway around the world.

Once upon a time, writers called for "process" shots, which meant that actors were photographed in front of projected images. The scenery outside a train or an automobile window looked flat and fake in comparison with the "original" subjects in the foreground. If the foreground is matted against a well-photographed background, the whole effect looks real even if foreground or background is actually a miniature.

If you have cable TV, you may occasionally view a half-hour program on the Discovery Channel called *Movie Magic*. A variety of experts prepare special effects for current movies—fires, earthquakes, building collapses, makeup and hairdo transformations, and so forth. *Movie Magic* also shows how stuntmen act as doubles for leading actors in dangerous situations. A few concealed wires and the matte process can make it possible for Tim Robbins to be seen falling from a forty-five-story building in the Coen brothers' *Hudsucker Proxy* (1994). But if the matte technique was an advance over the old process shot, the use of computers for digital effects is proving even more revolutionary. Weapons can be put in the hands of actors, empty theaters can be filled with spectators, and Forrest Gump can be made to shake hands with John Kennedy.

The preparation of the first answer print is not, however, the end of the production story. Today, as much as 100 percent of a movie's cost can be spent on *marketing*—the fifth step in the process—which is described in the next chapter.

7

Marketing

The marketing of a movie may begin with the purchase of the original story or the rights to film the life of a celebrity, or the signing of an actor or a director. The initial event will be followed by a series of publicity items intended to inform the public of its progress and make people eager to see the final result.

The movies—Hollywood style—have always been a commercial business and publicity has always been a mainstay of the production process. In the days of the major studios, every production had a unit publicity manager assigned to it. He, in turn, had a still photographer on hand to make a photographic record of the production so that magazines and newspapers would get adequate coverage. The bigger the budget (and thus the more important the project) the more people were assigned to generate public interest.

In the case of *Gone with the Wind*, for example, David Selznick hired a celebrated publicist named Russell Birdwell to handle the national campaign to find a suitable Scarlett O'Hara. The barrage of publicity continued long after Vivian Leigh, a relative unknown at the time, had been selected over such well-known beauties as Bette Davis, Paulette Goddard, and Joan Fontaine. Selznick also devised the technique known as saturation booking to squeeze the ultimate dollar out of all the publicity he had invested in his intended successor to *Gone with the Wind*, a less-than-successful Western with an all-star cast called *Duel in the Sun* (1946). Despite a cast that included Gregory Peck, Jennifer Jones, Joseph Cotten, Lionel Barrymore, Lillian Gish, Herbert Marshall, and others, he knew from previews that *Duel* might be a turkey, so he made 1,400 prints and opened the movie simultaneously in 1,400 theaters across the country. The first week's business, benefiting from the advance publicity, was sensational, but word-of-mouth kept people away in droves by the second week. Saturation technique is still in use. If there is built-in interest, saturate. If you have a sleeper with an unknown cast, open in a few key theaters, let the good word get around, and you can turn a modest effort into a hit without spending a fortune on marketing. If you've got *Batman* or a presold vehicle with Tom Cruise, such as *Mission: Impossible*, saturate. If it's a modest movie, imported from Australia or Italy, like *Shine* or *Life Is Beautiful*, depend on word-of-mouth.

In the old days, each of the major studios organized a yearly get-together of leading exhibitors (theater owners) and announced—with expensive publications, personal appearances by stars and starlets, and lots of good food and drink—the entire studio output for the coming year. This might include (for M-G-M in the thirties), in addition to the long-awaited *Mutiny on the Bounty* (1935), four as-yet-unnamed Clark Gable vehicles. It is important to remember that this method of marketing characterized the days of block booking. The theater owner could get *Mutiny on the Bounty* for his theater if he signed on for the other forty-plus movies, as well as for the shorts and newsreels that made up the M-G-M program. Four of the major studios—Paramount, M-G-M, Warner Bros., and Fox—also owned their own chain of theaters, which guaranteed release of the clinkers as well as the hot properties.

Once upon a time, the only revenue from movies came from theaters in which they were exhibited, in the United States and abroad. Today, there are many additional sources of income, and the growing prosperity of foreign countries, including those in the so-called Third World, has led to greater dependence on international markets for release in theaters and on TV, and on the burgeoning videotape market. (The two-part *Titanic* videotapes were widely publicized in the media in 1998 and were expected to sell more than 50 million copies, putting the previous best-seller, *The Lion King* [1994], in the boondocks.)

Today an independent filmmaker may finance his production by selling foreign rights for exhibition and video sales before he starts shooting. And there are movies that have a quick death at the theater box office but recoup their cost from television and videotape sales. I know of one Paramount production that cost a modest $5 million and would have required an additional investment of $7 million for advertising and prints if it had been given a national (U.S.) release. Paramount decided to swallow the production cost and shelve the movie, but not before booking it into an Arizona theater for a one-week run. That made the videotape and television sales of a "recent release" legitimate. And Paramount will get back its $5 million plus a small profit.

Disney must be considered the pioneer in movie marketing. Not only did "Uncle Walt" Disney foresee the value of his animated product for rerelease and sale to television, but he (or some of his henchmen) also had a very clear idea of how to get tie-ins of every production into the stores with a corresponding commission. In the early days it led to nothing more than children's books, dolls, and Mickey Mouse watches. Today, there are record albums, toys, sweaters, caps, T-shirts, and a dozen or more commercial outlets for the characters and props of *The Little Mermaid* (1989), *Aladdin* (1992), *Toy Story* (1995), and *Pocahontas* (1995). Revenue from the licensing of the long-haired Pocahontas doll could, for example, exceed revenue from the box office. And the profits from tie-ins is by no means limited to animated films. Models of characters and lethal objects from *Star Wars* (1977), the Indiana Jones (1981) movies, and *Star Trek* (1979), not to mention the very popular dinosaurs from *Jurassic Park* (1993), are veritable moneymaking machines. To what extent do considerations of peripheral profit influence the content of movies? Obviously, the influence is considerable. Steven Spielberg knew when he produced *Jurassic Park* that the tie-ins of his foray into dinosaurland would have enormous appeal for young people. And the certainty of profit on *Jurassic Park* minimized the financial risk (if there was any) on the grisly subject matter of *Schindler's List* (1993), his film about Nazi concentration camps.

But Spielberg is unique in using the profits from his marketwise production to pay for more risky but worthwhile ventures. Under the old studio system, it was quite possible for a studio to risk a few "noncommercial" projects, which would be paid for by surefire star-studded productions. There were even a few directors who would make deals with their studios to do a few commercial pieces in return for being allowed to do one risky art film. John Ford, for example, is said to have talked the studio head of RKO into letting him make *The Informer* (1935), an adaptation of a serious novel about Irish revolutionaries by Liam O'Flaherty, in exchange for an agreement to do a couple of potboilers. The fact that *The Informer* (written by Dudley Nichols) won several Academy Awards and, as a result, made some money was clearly unexpected.

No one knows exactly how much an Academy Award is worth in box office returns, but even a nomination can lead to extensive spending by producers in calling attention to this kind of recognition. And the amount of money spent by producers to influence the votes by Academy members is sometimes prodigious—just another example of the cost of marketing. While considering cost, it is essential to mention several factors that have made movies the expensive commodities they have become. The cost of talent, largely attributable to the increased influence of agents, is, of course, a major factor. Another cause, frequently cited by producers in their typical role as bosses, is the escalating cost of labor facilities, and equipment brought about by the rapid growth and strength of theatrical unions.

8

✛

On Criticism

One reason for writing a nontechnical book about the movies is to provide a few answers to the question "what do you think?" other than "wow!" or "it stinks." This doesn't mean that readers should become professional movie critics. But many of you are amateur movie critics already. Or you pretend to be. You see movies in theaters and may also see them at home—on late-night television broadcasts and on the tapes you rent from friendly video rental stores. And you offer words of wisdom about what you think and sometimes ask a lot of questions about the state of the art. What, you may ask, ever happened to musicals and Westerns? Should foreign films be dubbed or subtitled? How come some of us old-timers can't tell the difference between Sharon Stone and Demi Moore? And what about the Carradine brothers? Which one is the folk singer? You may discuss the relative merits of colorizing *Dark Victory* (1939)

or *The Maltese Falcon* (1941). Clearly, your tastes vary greatly.
And that's the fun of it. So what makes a movie a classic? Or
even "good" or "worth seeing"?

It is true that the theater critic of the *New York Times* can
make or break a play. But the same is not true for that venera-
ble publication's movie critics. Those involved in making a
movie (like the rest of us) crave affection and approval, and
this can be demonstrated in the press by kind words of praise
about performance, directing, acting, and writing. And certainly the publicity departments of the major distribution
companies, who are responsible for what they call "press
screenings," work very hard to create a favorable reaction for
every new feature they handle.

New York and Hollywood are the principal locales for the
presentation of new works. Most of the major companies in
Hollywood (what's left of them) have their own projection
rooms; some of the companies have screening rooms in their
New York headquarters. Others rent screening rooms of various sizes, depending on the nature of the movie. They
schedule a series of showings to accommodate the hundreds
of people credited. These include the representatives of the
local press, national magazines, syndicates, television, all
the radio commentators, and a lot of hangers-on with note-
books, cameras, and assorted paraphernalia, whose affiliations are questionable at best. Obviously, the company press
agents and the freelance public relations people who are
hired by independents are primarily concerned about critics
associated with major newspapers and magazines (e.g.,
Joseph Ansen of *Newsweek* and Richard Corliss and Richard
Schickel of *Time*), and, in this day and age, the critics with a
television following (e.g., Gene Shallit). It's not that public
relations folk can buy a good review with a lunch at "21" or
an intimate interview with Michelle Pfeiffer in her suite at
the Plaza, but such gestures help. Good movie critics tend to
be incorruptible, but that doesn't prevent the press agents
from trying. They have been known to preview new movies

on Caribbean islands, providing transportation and a three-day holiday to a select few.

When I was a practicing movie critic for *Life* and *Family Circle* magazines (1967–1971), I was invited to a screening or two every day. If I accepted these invitations (and I usually did), I would see over two hundred movies a year. Because I and other critics were inundated with screenings, because we received (and still do) hefty printed handouts of information about each movie, including lengthy synopses and biographies of everyone connected with the venture, sometimes including the hairdressers, we were naturally eager to "like" something. And after suffering through a batch of "dogs," we sometimes went off half-cocked with praise about a movie that was merely mediocre.

I have taught courses in practical film criticism, and students seem genuinely eager to practice critical writing on a subject in which they are definitely interested. The hardest thing to get students to do is to summarize succinctly what a movie is about (try it sometime) and to avoid the tendency to simply gush or throw up without giving a reason.

In the chapter on screenplays, I mentioned that plot premises give a clue to what a movie is about. Some people like to refer to plot premises as what-ifs. What if a man inherits a fortune, as in *Mr. Deeds Goes to Town* (1936)? Or, in *North by Northwest* (1959), what if a New York advertising man, intercepting a bellboy paging a Mr. Kaplan, is mistaken for Kaplan himself and is kidnapped?

Looking for the what-ifs or gimmicks in most of the movies we see can be fun. There was a piece in the Sunday *New York Times* a few years ago discussing the work of a hot new writer named Daniel Pyne, who had written a movie to star Michael J. Fox and James Woods called *The Hard Way* (1991). According to the article, "the movie . . . is a collision of characters built around a simple 'what if' premise. In this case, *what if* an intensely driven New York cop (Mr. Woods) hot on the trail of a serial killer is forced to baby-sit a pampered Hollywood movie star (Mr. Fox) who is out to research a role?"

As a moviegoer, you may find it useful to construct these succinct explanations of what a movie is about. If you can't do it, it may be because the movie isn't about *anything*. Or it may be that you don't know how to summarize.

In the same issue of the *New York Times* that gave the what-if of *The Hard Way*, film critic Caryn James contrasted two then current movies in two short sentences: "*Green Card* is about a strait-laced woman and a free-spirited man; *Pretty Woman* is about a free-spirited woman and a strait-laced man."

Subsequently, she narrowed it down to the common thread of mismatched couples who are thrown together—not a bad prerequisite for successful storytelling. Then, still sticking to the bare bones, she described Julia Roberts's role in *Pretty Woman* (1990) as "the wholesome streetwalker who captures the affection of a no-nonsense businessman." *Green Card* (1990) required a more complicated explanation: "[Gerard] Depardieu plays an up from the streets French composer who needs a green card and [Andie] MacDowell, a prim New York horticulturalist, wants an apartment with a greenhouse that will be given only to a married couple. They are then given forty-eight hours to become a convincing husband and wife, hoping to dupe snoopy immigration agents by memorizing the colors of each other's toothbrushes."

There are a few books on film criticism and quite a few anthologies of criticism by well-known critics: Otis Ferguson, James Agee, Pauline Kael, Stanley Kauffmann, Judith Crist, and Richard Schickel, to name a few. The New York Society of Film Critics once sponsored annual publications that were interesting for the fact that they published differing views of the same movie. The best book of this sort was *Film as Film* by Joy Gould Boyum and Adrienne Scott (now out of print), which gives the authors' views first and then contrasting reviews of a series of well-known movies, both foreign and domestic.

But the big question will always be, What did you think? And being able to give cogent reasons for your opinion will always be the essence of good criticism. All of this leads us to an exploration of various kinds of movies, some of which are far off the commercial beaten track.

9

About Animation

Animated cartoons can be considered the "purest" form of moviemaking because they derive entirely from images conceived and rendered by artists, not from the reproduction of elements in a real world. Movement itself is manipulated and since the late twenties has been magically wedded to lively and ingeniously created sound tracks. Animated short subjects were never box office bonanzas, even though their stars were frequently billed on marquees above the features they were intended to support. Thus the thirties belonged to Disney's Mickey Mouse and Donald Duck, the forties to Merrie Melodies' Bugs Bunny, and the fifties to a couple of upstarts from United Productions of America, the nearsighted Mr. Magoo and Gerald McBoing Boing, a precocious youngster (created by Dr. Seuss) who substituted sound effects for speech.

I am no animation expert, but I have written a lot of animation scripts, spending two and a half years with Disney and writing for thirty years thereafter (the most recent being a CBS presentation, *Gnomes*, in 1980). I can't draw, so I can't direct animation in the sense of supervising the preparation and shooting of backgrounds and the animation itself. But I have directed sound tracks for animation subjects, and it is customary to record the sound track before turning the project over to animators, since actions are drawn to match sounds. (This reverses the process of live action, in which the mix of sound tracks is the final process before printing.) This includes lip movement to match speech as well as physical movement to match footsteps, falls, slides, explosions, and so on.

A character can very easily be defined by the way he speaks, and his looks and movements will be governed by the voice and sounds recorded. This holds true even if a pretty little canary is drawn to match a deep bass voice.

There is a tradition in animation that versatile "voice men and women" can do anything. But I am a great believer in the idea of casting animation voices to type. I wrote a lot of cartoons for sponsors in which human characters were presented as animals or birds to avoid the possibility of offending anybody. After all, who wants to admit to looking like a donkey or a kangaroo? But how do you find the right voice for a donkey or a kangaroo? You close your eyes and listen. If a guy sounds like a donkey (even a mule) or a kangaroo, you cast him. If not, thank him and send him on his way.

Bear in mind that the animated cartoon appeared on film screens early on. Animated drawings actually preceded motion pictures. The old flip book could provide movement because of persistence of vision: The eye holds the impression of an image momentarily while it is replaced by another. The master physicist-lexicographer who is still credited with inventing the thesaurus, Peter Mark Roget, discovered persistence of vision in 1824. Almost a hundred years later, in 1911, a comic strip artist named Winsor McKay drew thousands of pictures of a dinosaur and put them on film to simulate movement. A few years later he traveled the country with his film as a vaudeville headliner. This is generally assumed to be the first successful theatrical presentation of animation in motion pictures. The filmed part of the act was called *Gertie the Dinosaur.*

The movie medium was made to order for the animator. Motion is achieved when a series of frames run intermittently through a projector at a number of frames a second (sixteen in the silent days, twenty-four with sound). Persistence of vision creates the illusion of motion even though what is being pr jected—however briefly—is a series of still pictures or drawings.

Although Winsor McKay made thousands of drawings to simulate real motion, some of his successors realized that even jerky motion could be interesting, so instead of sixteen drawings per second, they made twelve or even eight or fewer. Soon they figured out that they did not have to draw the background for each picture. The foreground character that moved could be on a separate celluloid transparency laid over a drawn background that did or did not move. And that character might only have to be redrawn in part to move some of his limbs but not the entire torso. If the figure was running or walking, only a few basic drawings were necessary because they could be repeated in cycles while the background moved behind him. Artists in the animation field were clever fellows who learned to present their images of simulated reality efficiently and effectively. What marks the difference between the simple matter of reproduction and genuine creative achievement is, in the last analysis, not the pretty picture but the content, although it's nice to have quality in both. New audiences may be enchanted by a drawn character such as a dinosaur that turns its head and then reaches up to bite into an apple, but after a while they demand that the character have an objective and that some other character try to interfere with that objective. They want a story.

When Walt Disney did his first synchronous-sound short subject, *Steamboat Willie* (1928), audiences were entranced by the synchronization of a stick producing the sounds of a xylophone by banging on the teeth of a cow and by Mickey's foot keeping perfect time to "Turkey in the Straw." But what made the cartoon work was that Mickey gave a boat ride to Minnie, that Peg Leg Pete tried to make out with her, and that Mickey saved her. And that was true of almost every cartoon Walt Disney ever made. They were often beautiful and they had good music. But they also had a simple story line as a basis for their gags and action. Donald Duck wants to spend a restful day at the beach but is harassed by an annoying bee. Two pretty trees stand side by side in a forest and love each other, but a jealous stump wants "in" and starts a forest fire to get his way. Two of the three little pigs submit to the entreaties of the big bad wolf and would have been eaten alive if not for the industrious third pig, who had the foresight to build his house of brick.

Lots of subjects that can be handled successfully in animation are not suitable at all for live action. Animation is a medium of miracles and should be used as such. It is also a wonderful medium for working with abstract ideas. Put a bubble over a character's head and show a green monster, and you have established greed. Make a character an owl and the audience will believe he is wise; a mule, and he is stubborn. Blind characters like Mr. Magoo can walk off the edge of a cliff and bounce back without realizing that anything unusual has happened. The Road Runner can be flattened to a pancake by a steamroller and be pulled back into shape by Bugs Bunny— anything is possible. Animation is a wild, wacky medium, and some very inventive minds have worked with it, including Dr. Suess, James Thurber, and Ray Bradbury.

The chief criticism leveled against Walt Disney was that he began, after the success of *Snow White and the Seven Dwarfs* (1937), to concentrate too heavily on technical improvement. He never abandoned his concern for story content and his fertile imagination was never satisfied with the first idea that came along. But he wanted to make animation lifelike. He succeeded so well in *Bambi* (1942), with his multiplane camera adding actual depth to the forest, that one wag wondered why he hadn't made the movie with real deer. By the time he made *Sleeping Beauty* (1959), his artists had improved their animation techniques to such a point that even the movements of human figures (always a bugaboo for animators) were fluid and natural. This was accomplished by using a rotoscope to trace photographed movement of real people. But was this lifelike achievement necessary?

One talented group of ex-Disney artists didn't think so. They left the studio after the 1941 strike for recognition of the Screen Cartoonists Guild. The strike had a traumatic effect on those who stayed as well as on those who struck, and it ended forever the "family spirit" that Walt tried so diligently to keep alive. Some of the staunch unionists (John Hubley and Phil Eastman) served in army motion picture units; others (Steve Bosustow, David Hilberman, and Zack Schwartz) formed an independent company (which became United Productions of America) and did some highly successful shorts for the armed forces on modest budgets, thus going into competition with their old boss and mentor (who relied on government contracts to shore up his shaky finances in the forties).

These ex-Disneyites saw the future of the medium in a return to individual expression unbounded by the constraints of realism. Or a lack of big budgets may have forced them to abandon the attempt at naturalism in favor of a stylization that was decidedly one-dimensional. They drew no elaborate sets. A nonexistent wall could be suggested by hanging one picture, a staircase by a bannister but no steps. The audience filled in the rest. This group, which called itself UPA, started on the "sponsored film" route with films for the armed forces, "message films" that led to the pro-Roosevelt *Hellbent for Election* paid for by the UAW/CIO as its contribution to Democratic candidates running for office in 1944. And then came *Brotherhood of Man* (1945), another United Auto Workers public service project, on which I (moonlighting without pay from my job at Disney) worked as one of the writers.

UPA's flat, stylized characters acting out stories against sketchy backgrounds more suggestive than real were clearly a reaction against Disney's trend toward lifelike reproduction, and their popularity led to a contract with Columbia Pictures. There, innovation led to literary adaptations of Ludwig Bemelman's charming children's classic, *Madeline,* James Thurber's *Unicorn in the Garden,* Edgar Allen Poe's *The Tell-Tale Heart,* and a freewheeling version of the Frankie and Johnny legend, *Rooty Toot Toot.*

Disney had dominated the cartoon field for twenty years, winning dozens of Oscars. But most of the Academy Awards for animation in the early fifties went to UPA for McBoing Boing, Magoo, and company. Some of Disney's artists, notably the talented Ward Kimball (who headed a jazz combo of Disneyites called the Firehouse Five that did professional gigs around town), went to Walt and asked for permission to do a little avant-garde animation (anyone who has seen the "Pink Elephants" number from *Dumbo* [1941] needs no proof of Disney artists' capabilities in this sphere). The result was a unique cartoon in Cinemascope—*Toot, Whistle, Plunk, and Boom*—done in the flat UPA style, only better; it was the Academy Award winner for 1953. Kimball triumphantly approached Disney the day after the award with an idea for a follow-up. "Forget it," Walt said. "We've proved we can do it. Now let's get back to what we do best."

UPA, with Gerald McBoing Boing and Mr. Magoo, thrived for a couple of years. Then, like Mickey Mouse and other distinguished predecessors, it was gobbled up by the mass production of television programming, which includes the Saturday-morning kiddie shows, many of them produced overseas (especially in the Far East) at a lower cost than is possible in the United States. Disney has until recently remained aloof from this trend. It even has its own cable network to parcel out gems from its ample and very rich library. But what was once a great creative incubator in the film industry has turned into a vast corporate enterprise. One of its recent products, *Toy*

Story (1995), is the work of computer technicians, not graphic artists. The master is dead. The company is in new hands and is one of the most successful in Hollywood. But the old magic, in my opinion, is gone.

In the next chapter we consider another type of movie—the nonfiction film or documentary.

10

Nonfiction

The introduction of the documentary as a feature film attraction is usually attributed to Robert Flaherty's *Nanook of
the North*, which was successfully distributed worldwide in
1922 by Pathe. Originally financed as a promotional piece by a
fur company, Revillon Frères, it told the story of one Eskimo
family and its struggle to survive during the four seasons of
the year in the Arctic. Some of the so-called real-life incidents,
such as building an igloo and struggling with a seal, were
staged or reenacted, but the shots of the snow-covered Arctic
wasteland were genuine. Flaherty's camera (engineered by
Eastman Kodak to operate at below-freezing temperatures)
actually did record walrus hunts, fishing, and a spectacular
Arctic blizzard. The success of *Nanook* (which opened at the
Capitol Theater in New York on a double bill with Harold
Lloyd's *Grandma's Boy*) led others to try their hand at feature
documentaries. Merian C. Cooper and Ernest Schoedsack

(later to have a great success with *King Kong* [1933]) made two nonfiction features that were distributed by Paramount. *Grass* (1925) was about the perilous migration of Bakhtaran tribesmen through Persia and Turkey to find suitable pastures for their herds. *Chang* (1927), the more successful of the two, repeated the formula of *Nanook* with a family struggling to survive, this time a Siamese family in the jungles of Thailand facing attacks by predatory animals and a devastating stampede by a herd of elephants (the *Chang* of the title). Later came several African safari movies, some by a noted circus lion tamer, Frank Buck, and a few more by a husband-and-wife team, Martin and Osa Johnson. Admiral Richard Byrd's historic trip to the South Pole was photographed and released as a feature, *With Byrd at the South Pole* (1930). Another documentary of man's struggle against natural challenges was the feature-length record of a difficult mountain climb—*Annapurna* (1950).

None of these films was a smashing box office success (the most profitable documentary to date is *Hoop Dreams* [1994]), but the early documentaries got bookings around the world and made profits for their sponsors. The pioneer, Robert Flaherty, was signed by Jesse Lasky of Paramount to make a sequel to *Nanook*, this time in the South Pacific. It was called *Moana of the South Seas* (1926) and was promoted widely with pictures of beautiful native girls in sexy poses. The advertising was misleading. The film was an honest portrait of an island paradise (Tahiti), beautifully photographed but lacking *Nanook*'s drama of humankind against a hostile environment.

Soviet Russia developed a movie industry that was far removed from Hollywood but had a profound influence on the evolution of the documentary film. Lenin was the first national leader to recognize that the moving picture could be a major force in molding public opinion. His successful Communist takeover in 1917 had to be sold to the Russian masses. He commissioned young Russian filmmakers to do the job and used the authority of a socialist state to set up schools to train future filmmakers. Out of this cauldron of state support came a rich legacy of exciting, experimental filmmaking (most of it dedicated to selling the revolution to the Russian people) that, in terms of technique, was extremely influential in Western countries. Names of filmmakers such as Pudovkin, Dovchenko, Eisenstein, and Vertov were known internationally. Eisenstein's *The Battleship Potemkin,* made in 1925, re-created a mutiny by Russian sailors against the czarist fleet off Odessa in 1905. It was an early example of *docudrama,* which is based on history. *Potemkin* includes one of the most celebrated sequences in the history of movies—the "Odessa Steps"—more than 400 shots of czarist troops advancing on and slaughtering civilians.

A young Scottish prelate named John Grierson was deeply impressed by the effectiveness of Soviet films like *Potemkin.* And it was he, more than anyone else, who sold the idea of informational, persuasive movies called documentaries to the Western world. He needed funding for his experiment in movies, and he was a superlative salesman and an astute politician. He got the financial support of the Empire Marketing Board in London, attracted a corps of young men of leftist leanings to work with him, and began to turn out what were essentially promotional films about Great Britain, its products, its people, and its institutions.

Drifters (1929), his first film—and the only one for which he is credited as director—was about the herring industry. There followed films about the international tea trade (*Song of Ceylon* [1934]), about British craftsmen (*Industrial Britain* [1933]), and about communications (*Night Mail* [1936]). His group of Young Turks even made a film for the gas, light, and coke monopoly that we know as *Housing Problems* (1935). This film used synchronous sound for the first time to interview residents of old housing in London.

What Grierson demonstrated was that documentary, nonfiction films could "say" something. Since he began his filmmaking career at a time when sound was just being introduced, a lot of what these films "said" was conveyed by narration, but they were skillfully made and edited, and many had original musical scores by Britain's leading composers. *Night Mail*, with a score by Benjamin Britten, even had as narration a poetic text written by a leading poet, W. H. Auden.

The result of this new and often didactic approach to the documentary form was bound to have an influence around the world, and it did. It gave rise to the social documentary in the United States, and it led to the widespread use of film by the Nazis.

Many students of film history are familiar with two famous nonfiction U.S. films of the thirties—*The River* (1937) and *The City* (1939). But every film student has heard of and perhaps has seen the infamous but brilliant *Triumph of the Will* (1934), directed by Leni Riefenstahl, celebrating the 1934 Nazi congress at Nuremberg for her sponsor, Adolph Hitler.

Riefenstahl, now in her nineties, has spent a lifetime belittling the stigma of her Nazi past. She had been an actress, an underwater photographer, and an anthropologist of sorts and claims that she was merely recording an event at Nuremberg. It is true that there is no narration in her film of the Nazi congress. But her cameras focused admiringly on Hitler and his colleagues, and their blatant claims to the rebirth of the German spirit are recorded in full. This raises the question (always answered in the negative) of whether a factual film can ever be totally objective.

The thirties brought about a radical change in the objectives of the independent filmmakers, who have always been the principal users of movies for the presentation of ideas—personal or political. These were troubled times marked by worldwide depression and the growth of Fascism in Europe and in Asia. Even artists began to substitute social purpose for aesthetic experiment. In the United States, people like Paul Strand and Ralph Steiner, who had made avant-garde films in the twenties, helped to organize the leftist Film and Photo League, which gave birth to Nykino and later became

Frontier Films. They brought together writers, cameramen, editors, actors, and musicians who, while pursuing establishment careers to earn their keep, were willing to work extra hours to produce significant subjects that the establishment wouldn't touch.

Some Film and Photo League projects are still available. *Pie in the Sky* (1935) can be rented from the Museum of Modern Art. It includes an appearance by Elia Kazan, later to be a successful Hollywood director and a controversial figure who endorsed the industry-wide blacklist by giving names to the House Un-American Activities Committee. The Museum of Modern Art also has rental copies of the *Workers' Newsreels*, which were released monthly to present material not available in the news releases of the major companies. Left-wing in tone, these films were not run in theaters controlled by Hollywood, and there were few cine-clubs in the United States to facilitate distribution of antiestablishment material.

President Hoover, with his famous (and easily refuted) slogan "Prosperity is just around the corner," considered the Depression a temporary condition. So was his presidency. He was replaced in 1933 by Franklin D. Roosevelt with his optimistic assertion that "The only thing we have to fear is fear itself." But the crisis in confidence continued. Most newspapers were strictly Republican. Radio was bland— news reporting did not mature until the international scene became acutely dangerous. Movies, for the most part, were in their escapist phase. Only gangster films seemed real. Newsreels, by design, avoided controversy. But workers were getting militant. There was the beginning of industrial unionism and a new organization—the Congress of Industrial Organizations (CIO). There were hunger marches. Thousands of unemployed World War I veterans marched on Washington, D.C., to demand early payment of a promised bonus. The shanties they built outside town were finally destroyed by troops under General Douglas MacArthur (despite President Hoover's orders to the contrary). Left-wing independents made movies of these events, which were shown in cine-clubs—halls, union headquarters, and so forth.

There were also major problems on the international front. Japan invaded Manchuria in 1931, Mussolini was rattling his sabers with the idea of annexing Austria, and the Nazis controlled Germany. The U.S. government, probably reflecting the dominant view of its isolationist citizens, took a neutral position. The United States, including American Jews, largely ignored the Nazi threat, despite official Nazi anti-Semitism. But I spent five days in Berlin on the way back from the Soviet Union in 1934, and I saw what Soviet friends had alerted me to, that Nazism was synonymous with militarism and would inevitably lead to aggression. Indeed, Hitler had made it clear in *Mein Kampf* that Germany was entitled to *Lebensraum* (living space). Many in the United States (as well as the socialist authors H. G. Wells and George Bernard Shaw in Britain) had considered Fascism in Mussolini's Italy benevolent. After all, the trains in Italy ran on time. But Engelbert Dollfuss, the chancellor of Austria, was assassinated while I was in the Soviet Union in the summer of 1934, followed by serious threats from the Italians to march on Vienna. But the real preview for the world war that was to come began in 1936 when a Spanish general, Francisco Franco, launched an attack on the duly elected Republic of Spain. (Alphonso XIII, the hemophiliac Hapsburg monarch of Spain, had abdicated a few years before.) Both Italy and Nazi Germany openly aided Franco, whereas France, Britain, and the United States, to their everlasting shame, observed strict neutrality. The Soviets sent many advisers and insufficient aid. International brigades were organized by volunteers from many uncommitted countries, as well as from the Soviet Union and Germany. In 1937 Italy annexed Ethiopia. In 1938, when Hitler threatened to take over the Sudetenland, Neville Chamberlain and Edouard Daladier, the prime ministers of Britain and France, respectively, flew to Munich to meet with Hitler and Mussolini and came away with the pact that gave the Sudetenland to Hitler, prompted Chamberlain's fallible proclamation that he had achieved "peace in our time," and gave birth to what we have known ever since as "appeasement."

These troubled times were fertile years for the nonfiction film. Why? Because documentaries thrive on trouble. You can't make successful documentaries about the best of all possible worlds. The most successful documentaries have always thrived on adversity. Consider *Nanook* (man against the hostile forces of nature), *Annapurna* (man conquering an insurmountable peak), *With Byrd at the South Pole,* and so forth.

In the United States we had the Depression. We had unemployment, the dustbowl, floods on the Mississippi. We also had a young movie critic named Pare Lorentz, who happened to meet a member of FDR's New Deal brain trust, Rexford Guy Tugwell, then head of the Resettlement Administration. Lorentz talked Tugwell into sponsoring a film about the dustbowl. Lorentz was ideal for this job—liberal but not completely left. His objective was to call for social awareness rather than change.

There had been government films in the United States before, but they were intended for government employees—information, training, morale building, and so forth. The film Lorentz proposed (which would be *The Plow That Broke the Plains* [1936]) was intended for the general public.

Never having made a film, he turned to skilled independents for help. He was familiar with the work of Nykino and the Film and Photo League and signed up Paul Strand, Leo Hurwitz, and Ralph Steiner. He had no script but, in the best documentary tradition, he had a problem—how the sun and wind had ravaged the grass of the plains. And if he offered no solution, he would make audiences *think*. His filmmakers took a more radical stance. It wasn't the forces of nature that had destroyed the land, they said. It was exploitation by man. Greed! The free enterprise system!! Steiner told me that he had not been part of the controversy. It is certainly possible that

Lorentz agreed with his filmmakers' leftist views, but he had to temper them to fulfill his obligation to his government sponsors. He was advocating conservation, not social reform. But there is no question that in the famous "wheat for the war" sequence in *The Plow* he shows how the land was exploited for profit.

With a minuscule budget of $15,000 for *The Plow That Broke the Plains,* he had counted on using footage from Hollywood films to give some historical background to the dust bowl crisis. But Hollywood's brass shut the door on him. They didn't want to help the government go into the movie business, though a few years later—after Pearl Harbor—their attitude changed completely.

Since Lorentz was familiar with Grierson's work in Britain, he recognized the value of using the best available talent for music and narration. He induced the noted American composer and music critic Virgil Thomson to do the score for *The Plow,* employing familiar American folk themes. The score was subsequently recorded and played in a symphonic version by orchestras around the country. A distinguished Metropolitan Opera baritone, Thomas Chalmers, was the narrator. And then Lorentz found out that the major film companies, which had refused to supply stock footage and which controlled most U.S. movie theaters, wouldn't show his film. One exhibitor, Arthur Mayer (who later taught film history at Dartmouth and became my mentor), booked it at his Rialto Theater (famous as the "house of horror") in New York's Times Square. Mayer billed it as "the picture they dared us to show." It was a success with audiences and ultimately ran in 3,000 theaters across the country. Consequently, Lorentz was asked by the government to produce a second film, this time with a respectable budget, full support, and distribution by Paramount Pictures. It was what many consider to be the best narrated documentary ever made in the United States—*The River* (1937).

In this second attempt, Lorentz is far less scrupulous in not attacking capitalist exploitation, as is indicated by the oft repeated line: "We built a thousand cities and a thousand towns, but at what a cost!" On *The River* Lorentz worked from a script. The narration, in the vein of a Carl Sandburg poem, is full of American names. This is, after all, the story of the greatest river in the land—the Mississippi—and what happened to the heartland of America adjacent to it and to its tributaries. The text was again read by the mellifluent Thomas Chalmers and the music composed by Virgil Thomson.

Lorentz's films were made for the Resettlement Administration, which was subsequently declared unconstitutional. President Roosevelt, however, was so impressed by *The River* that he proposed that the government set up a U.S. Film Service with Lorentz as its chief. This would make it possible for the Film Service to make films for all agencies of the government. Unfortunately, Republicans viewed government filmmaking as New Deal propaganda and, with the imminence of war, film funds were cut off. FDR, now busy seeking aid for Britain, did not fight to have the appropriation restored.

The U.S. documentary movement, which got a boost from Lorentz's government-sponsored projects, got an even stronger boost from the popularity of a variety of films at the 1939 New York World's Fair, notably from the success of *The City*, shown at the pavilion of its sponsor, the American Institute of Planners. It was made by two veterans of the old left-wing independent movement—Willard Van Dyke and Ralph Steiner—and, with realism and wit, it showed how the city had disintegrated since colonial times, offering hope for the future in a climactic section shot in a planned greenbelt community in New Jersey. Ever since, big world's fairs have been a major source of funding for unusual nonfiction films, often introducing new technology as well as new techniques. The biggest hit of the New York World's Fair in the early sixties was *To Be Alive* (1965), a multiscreen tribute to humankind by Francis Thompson and Alexander Hammid. The major attractions at Montreal's Expo of 1967 were films of one sort or another—multiscreen, wraparound, rotating, and so forth. But *The City* used no new technology. It simply showed more imagination in picture and sound than had been seen in U.S. documentary up to that time—including something that had been noticeably lacking in Lorentz's movies and the workers' movies, namely, humor.

The City also illustrated the fatal flaw of most sponsored films: the presentation of a problem is often valid and effective, but the solution—the sponsor's message—may be dubious indeed. The best of intentions go down the drain with unacceptable platitudes and treacle. The garden city offered as an alternative to the exciting but grisly metropolis in *The City* seems pallid and unreal.

Remember that *The City* appeared in 1939—the year of the Nazi–Soviet pact, which was followed by the invasion of Poland and the beginning of World War II in September. The buildup to and the outbreak of World War II, even more than the Depression, proved an important breeding ground for the nonfiction film. In the United States the people who had organized themselves into the Film and Photo League to deal with domestic issues took the lead in making films about international problems as well. The same Herbert Kline who had been involved with *Pie in the Sky* made *Heart of Spain* (1937) about Dr. Norman Bethune—a Canadian society physician who gave up his Montreal practice to help the Spanish Loyalists and organized the first mobile blood bank. Kline (who died in early 1999) also produced *Crisis* (1938), about the disintegration of Czechoslovakia after the Munich pact, and *Lights Out in Europe* (1940), about the fall of Poland. The former included commentary by noted war correspondent Vincent Sheean (*Personal History*), the latter by British novelist James Hilton (*Goodbye Mr. Chips*). One of the best known anti-Fascist films of the thirties was made by the respected Dutch documentarist Joris Ivens, *The Spanish Earth* (1937), for which Ernest Hemingway, then a staunch supporter of Spain's Republican cause, wrote the script and narration. The film was sponsored by leading American intellectuals and artists and was shown at fund-raising affairs for the Spanish Loyalists around the United States and elsewhere. Ivens also worked with Herbert Kline on a film about the Japanese threat in the Far East called *The Four Hundred Million* (1938). It was sympathetic to the Chinese Communist Eighth Route Army and countered the prevalent notion that Chiang Kai-shek was the savior of China.

All of these films were produced independently while Hollywood, despite the dominant role that Jewish Americans played in controlling content, ignored the threat of Fascism. The attack on Pearl Harbor and our declaration of war in December 1941 changed all that. The prevalence of isolationist, pacifist thinking had to be overcome, and film was to be used as a principal weapon. There ensued a widespread mobilization of movie talent to do what it could do best: make movies. Writers, producers, and directors who were accustomed to turning out escapist fiction entertainment had to adapt themselves to nonfiction. The objective was to explain why we were fighting and to whip up patriotism and support for our allies—including the previously hated Russians. Some of the films, including Hollywood director Frank Capra's famous *Why We Fight* series (1943), are such flagrant propaganda that they are embarrassing to see today. But those were the days when General Douglas MacArthur could say, "The hopes of civilization ride on the banners of the glorious Red Army."

To the British—whose homeland was hit by Nazi bombs after the fall of France—the war was already a battle for survival. Fortunately, they had developed (under Grierson) a skilled corps of documentary filmmakers who moved over from the General Post Office sponsorship to the Crown Film Unit and started making morale-building films and films for international consumption—especially in the United States—that would help win support for their cause. The message of the first British films was "we can take it," showing the courage of the people under fire, their dedication to war work, and their sacrifice—typical "stiff upper lip" stuff. One film was actually called *London Can Take It* (1940). This certainly created sympathy abroad, but not confidence. So within a year and a half, the message switched to "we can dish it out." And you had films like *Target for Tonight* (1941), which chronicled a successful RAF raid on Germany.

The Army Signal Corps, by tradition a military branch concerned with communication, had the major job of making orientation and training films for the GIs. The West Coast head of the Signal Corps was a producer named Sam Briskin, who was then designated a colonel, as were most of the producers who joined the armed forces.

The Office of War Information was established, and an ex-newspaperman named Lowell Mellett set up shop in Hollywood to advise studios on useful war-supportive subjects as well as to goose the studios into making them. This office also worked out a deal with the distributing companies to include government-made propaganda films in theaters.

(One piece of information worth noting and seldom mentioned is that the movie industry, unlike any other in the country, served the war effort in many ways without being reimbursed—even on a cost-plus basis. In this connection, they produced 16 millimeter prints of feature films and made them available to military bases and ships at sea free of charge. This generous gesture opened the way for a profitable postwar market for the distribution of films on 16 millimeter, a new market that prospered for many years until the wide acceptance of films on videotape.)

No war up to that time had been covered so completely by movie cameras. One film, *The True Glory* (1945)—a joint British-American project with two directors: Garson Kanin (U.S.) and Carol Reed (British) and not released until after the surrender of Germany—included the work of 1,400 Allied cameramen, 101 of whom were wounded and 32 killed. Steven Spielberg, director and producer of *Saving Private*

Ryan, used twenty minutes of film time to re-create the landing on Omaha Beach, but *The True Glory* shows the real thing.

One effect of movies that show war with stark realism is that they tend to become a statement against war. (Being antiwar was undoubtedly the goal of *Saving Private Ryan,* but having a contemporary embodiment of Private Ryan salute the white cross marking the grave of the fallen Captain Miller at the end of the Spielberg movie conveys quite the opposite message.) When the army brass saw director John Huston's film about the Italian campaign, *The Battle of San Pietro* (1945), which not only included grim shots of battle but a painful scene of burial and of hundreds of white crosses, they thought it was antiwar. Told that the film might not be released, Huston is said to have replied, "When the day comes that I make a movie that is *for* war, I ought to be taken out and shot." Nevertheless, the army added a prologue in which General Mark Clark explains the importance of the Italian campaign to justify the sacrifice of human life. No such simple solution was found for the release of another Huston army documentary, *Let There Be Light* (1946), made in the Sawtelle, California, Veterans Administration hospital to show—quite positively, as a matter of fact—the postwar psychological rehabilitation of brain-damaged GIs. The army refused to let that film be shown publicly until a few years ago.

But there has never been a time like that of World War II in which the documentary played a role of such importance. It was the visual supplement to the major communications medium of the era, the radio, which brought us analysis of day-to-day events, eyewitness accounts of battles and bombings, and all of Hitler's major speeches—and Churchill's as well. Later, this material would find its way onto film as the documentary began to assume its place as the predominant medium for recording history.

11

Television

After the war, the birth and rapid growth of a new medium—television—seemed made to order for the distribution of informational subject matter. The new medium had an enormous appetite for any kind of visual broadcast material, and in order to obtain a license for the use of free airwaves (in other words, to lay legitimate claim to a valuable TV channel) the licensed stations were obliged to broadcast a minimum amount of useful educational material. This arrangement would, it seemed, open a vast new distribution market for the documentary filmmaker.

What was unfortunate about the period—and I speak of the fifties, when documentaries might have attracted large audiences on television—is that it coincided with what we know as the McCarthy era, a period of very stringent thought control. Anyone associated with dissent was actually barred from employment—in movies, on television, and in the schools.

And for the most part, people who make documentaries have always been dissenters who are outside the establishment. But many of the army and navy recruits who had been drawn into moviemaking for the first time during the war wanted to continue working in the movie medium but had no connections in Hollywood, which was where the "action" was. The result was that a large group from the Long Island branch of the Signal Corps—which had used the old Paramount facilities in Astoria—went across the East River to Manhattan and used their newfound skills to make films for sponsors as well as commercials for the infant television industry.

Television should have been a bonanza for the documentary filmmaker. But it didn't turn out that way, despite the obligation placed on networks and stations to provide socially useful, educational material. What the major networks did was schedule the "serious stuff" on Sundays and early, creating what became known as the "Sunday ghetto." Despite this obvious discrimination against socially useful programming, the networks did manage in this period before public broadcasting to produce some interesting documentary material, but it was for the most part not controversial. Not that it was uninteresting. The NBC series *Victory at Sea* (1952) was skillfully edited from World War II naval footage by Henry Salomon and Ike Kleinerman and included a score by noted composer Richard Rodgers. (It is still being used on the airwaves today.)

To carry out their public-service obligation, the networks ran many profiles of famous people, biographies of historical figures, and accounts of events from history. (*You Are There* looked at events such as the assassination of Julius Caesar as it might be reported by a modern news team.) CBS's *Omnibus* program dealt with art, music, and literature and presented documentaries on aspects of American life. Because U.S. audiences are drawn to "names," television developed the narrator star. CBS had Edward R. Murrow and later Walter Cronkite. There was Chet Huntley at NBC, where the current events series was called the *NBC White Paper*; at ABC it was called (and still is, when they do one) *Close-Up*, with Frank McGee and sometimes David Brinkley as host and narrator.

But television, in the fifties, was as cautious about controversial issues as the movie industry was. After all, it was under sharp surveillance by the lunatic fringe of the extreme right. With its income dependent on the goodwill of advertisers who were the bigwigs of corporate America, television was not going to lead the fight against thought control resulting from McCarthyism. Nevertheless, it was a television program that helped bring about the demise of McCarthy himself, even though it did not end the inquisition attached to his name. It was one of the *See It Now* series, which featured Edward R. Murrow and was produced by Fred Friendly. It was presented on CBS, which was not exactly known for standing up to the inquisition. CBS had, in fact, instituted its own loyalty oath to comply with the anti-Communist spirit of the times. And Murrow was a CBS vice president. But *See It Now* had already taken a stand against unsubstantiated red-baiting on two of its programs—*The Case against Milo Radulovich* and *Argument at Indianapolis* (both in 1953). The *See it Now* program on McCarthy was daring because it was a direct attack on the sacred cow of anti-Communism and used footage of McCarthy himself to build a case against his methods. McCarthy was outraged and demanded equal time. He got it and was so ineffective that his prestige with the public was forever damaged.

(It should be made clear that Joseph McCarthy, a first-term senator from Wisconsin, headed the Senate Government Operations Committee and its subcommittee on investigations, whose inquisitorial functions were directed against parts of the government engaged in international activities—the State Department, for example, and the U.S. Information Agency, which established libraries of U.S. literature around the world, including the works of such "subversives" as John Steinbeck and John Dos Passos. The House Un-American Activities Committee, on the other hand, could harass alleged domestic rascals like actors, screenwriters, and teachers.)

See It Now scored a stunning propaganda victory over the senator from Wisconsin, but he was actually undone by his own party, which no longer benefited from his underhanded attacks on Democrats and liberals. Once Dwight Eisenhower, a Republican, was in the White House, McCarthy's usefulness to his party was finished. Besides, Ike hated the bullying senator and everything he stood for. Thus when McCarthy made the mistake of charging that there was a red plot in the army (the countercharge was that he launched the attack because his young cronies, Roy Cohn and David Schine, had been denied commissions), the televised hearings with army lawyer Joseph Welch spouting his famous line, "Have you no decency?" finally did him in and led to a subsequent Senate censure. McCarthy died in 1957 at the age of forty-eight of cirrhosis of the liver.

I first became fully aware of the CBS network's willingness to cope with major issues in 1959. That was the year of *Harvest of Shame*, a stinging *CBS Reports* indictment of the East Coast system that exploited migrant farm workers. Ed R. Murrow narrated (it was one of his last assignments before leaving CBS for the USIA), and he concluded with these pertinent remarks:

> The migrants have no lobby. Only an enlightened, aroused and perhaps angered public opinion can do anything about the migrants. The people you have seen have the strength to harvest your fruit and vegetables. They do not have the strength to influence legislation. Perhaps we do. Good night and good luck.

Each of the major networks now entered the news-documentary field with controversial subjects. ABC did a useful environmental piece as part of its *Close-Up* series. It was called *Who Killed Lake Erie?* (1969). The NBC *White Paper* series included an attack on illegal gambling called *Biography of a Bookie Joint* (1961) and subsequently took a stab at desegregation with *Walk in My Shoes*.

It so happened that this transformation of TV documentary coincided with a revolutionary technological development in the filming of these subjects—the use of portable sync-sound recording equipment and cameras. Lightweight 16 millimeter cameras—principally the Arriflex—had been developed by the Germans during World War II, and the Allies were quick to seize them. The Arriflex was a wonderful instrument for recording actual events in the field. It could easily be carried with a 400-foot magazine, which would permit covering a subject or an incident for ten minutes of film time. And the Swiss had developed a remarkably efficient piece of equipment for recording sound on quarter-inch magnetic tape—the Naggra tape recorder. The quality of sound on quarter-inch tape was equal to that obtained on magnetic film, which had replaced prewar photoelectric recording systems that made sound on film possible. The problem for documentary filmmakers was that to achieve synchronous sound (in other words, speech) the new lightweight cameras had to be connected to the new lightweight recording equipment by means of a coaxial cable, which meant that the cameraman and soundman were tied together. This greatly hampered the mobility needed to cover active scenes.

Finally a group of East Coast documentary filmmakers figured out how to use pieces of crystal to create a pulse to synchronize camera and recorder even if they were not directly connected. The new system, as far as I know, was first used in 1959 to make a filmed record of the Kennedy–Humphrey Democratic primary in Wisconsin. The film was called, appropriately enough, *Primary* (1960) and was broadcast on ABC as the first of a notable series of so-called cinema verité subjects produced by Drew Associates, who were then under contract to Time Incorporated. Four of the filmmakers on *Primary*—Albert Maysles, Ricky Leacock, Donn Pennebaker, and Bob Drew himself—would go their separate ways in a few years, but each became a noted and respected exponent of what they preferred to call "direct cinema," not cinema verité, because each of them admitted—in a variety of public statements—that although the intention of their work was to be as objective as possible, true objectivity was impossible, given the point of view of the man behind the camera, the sound recordist, and, ultimately, the editor.

The sixties, a period of great social unrest, was covered in various ways by the Drew group and others, beginning with the Cuban missile crisis, which even attracted a French documentary filmmaker, Chris Marker, the result being his film *Cuba Si!* (1961).

One of the most celebrated works of the Drew group was *Crisis: Beyond a Presidential Commitment* (1963), which was shot by two crews—one in the White House with the Kennedys and one in Alabama with Governor George Wallace to record his famous confrontation with Nicholas Katzenbach when the latter sought to enforce the laws against segregation by accompanying two blacks through the portals of the University of Alabama.

Meanwhile, NBC began to promote and develop its *Project 20* series under the able and creative hand of Don Hyatt, who got his first job with the new NBC documentary unit after graduation from Dartmouth and learned the trade under the tutelage of Henry Salomon on the *Victory at Sea* (1952) series. When Salomon died in 1957, Hyatt took over the unit. His *Project 20* was unique among documentary programs in that it had, for some time, a bona fide commercial sponsor (Lincoln National Life) and it was shown on prime time (in the evening). For the most part, the series (with one show a month) avoided controversy in favor of historical subjects such as *Meet Mr. Lincoln* (1959) and *The Real West* (1961), and biblical visualizations such as *The Coming of Christ* (1960) and *The Law and the Prophets* (1967). But a program called *Nightmare in Red China* (1955), a belated attack on Bolsheviks and the Russian Revolution (put together with a compilation of old footage), created enough of a stir to call for an anti-Nazi follow-up, *The Twisted Cross* (1956).

Hyatt and his associates understood, however, that to attract prime-time audiences to documentary required the use of "names" in one capacity or another. Thus some of the best and most informative subjects like *The Real West* and *The End of the Trail* (1967) included movie stars such as Gary Cooper and Walter Brennan on camera and as narrators. (Both of these subjects were done on an animation stand with the "stills-in-motion" technique that brought still photographs to life—something Ken Burns has done in his Civil War, baseball, and Jefferson subjects for PBS but without acknowledging the groundbreaking work of his predecessors.)

After the Public Broadcasting Service (PBS) got a foothold in most big cities, the networks cut back on their nonfiction coverage, leaving documentaries almost entirely to the new broadcasting system. And PBS has, until the recent cutbacks in its government subsidy, responded well to its responsibility with science *(Nova)*, nature *(Wild America* and *Nature)*, social issues *(Frontline)*, and a variety of independently produced subjects like those of Frederick Wiseman *(Welfare Center* [1975] and *Model* [1980]) and Allen and Susan Raymonds's *Police Tapes* (1978), as well as the more recent *The Thin Blue Line* (1988), *Roger and Me* (1989), *Hoop Dreams* (1994), and the well-regarded offerings by Ken Burns.

One problem is that documentary filmmakers are forced to spend more time raising money for their projects than they do on the creative process. Barbara Kopple, who completed the Academy Award–winning film *Harlan County, U.S.A.* in 1976, spent five years on the project, shooting it in fits and starts as money became available. PBS helps finance a few of these films and buys a few for presentation after they are completed, but, unfortunately, the most active documentary filmmakers are those who can write the most effective grant proposals.

In the fifties, there were a few documentaries that made it in theaters—*Kon Tiki* (1951), Jacques Cousteau's *The Silent World* (1956), *The Eleanor Roosevelt Story* (1965), and a series of popular Disney *True Life Adventures* (*Seal Island* [1948], *Beaver Valley* [1950]), which infuriated nature purists because they inevitably featured cutesy anthropomorphism synchronized to musical scores. Cousteau's under-water features, on the other hand, were used as the pattern for his widely accepted television show.

The sixties ushered in the era of the filmed rock musical for theater release, including a portrait of Dylan on a British tour, *Don't Look Back* (1967); the Maysles brothers' *Gimme Shelter*, a film about a U.S. Rolling Stones tour (1970); and *Woodstock* (1970), one of the highest grossing documentaries of all time, the chronicle of a memorable hippie gathering in upstate New York that also included two hours of big-name rock performances. *Monterey Pop* (1969), about another rock festival, played theaters with less impact. Rock documentaries, which include extensive footage of performances, continue to be made, a recent example being Madonna's revealing self-portrait, *Truth or Dare* (1991).

As for nonmusical documentaries, it is worth noting that one subject, *Salesman* (1969), by the gifted Maysles brothers, Albert and David, actually played Radio City Music Hall. Marcel Ophüls's four-hour examination of France during the Nazi occupation, *The Sorrow and the Pity* (1970), had a successful run in art theaters, as did Claude Lanzmann's nine-hour *Shoah* (1986), attendance at which became somewhat obligatory for Jews, who had been deeply affected by the Holocaust. Ophüls's *Hotel Terminus*, a lengthy but well-constructed account of the search for alleged concentration camp butcher Klaus Barbie, was shown at the New York Film Festival in 1992 but did little business at the box office.

Documentaries that win Oscars are almost always about problems, often about the lame, the halt, and the blind, about old age and illness, and, in recent years, very often about the dreadful consequences of AIDS. For a time, it was possible to predict the documentary Oscar winner if the nominations included an entry about a blind man or a one-armed basketball player or, as happened one year, about a retarded man of middle age, *Best Boy* (1979). There is really nothing wrong with this phenomenon. It is very difficult, as I have noted, to make nonfiction films about the best of all possible worlds. Documentary is a medium for calling attention to our problems and weaknesses. For this reason, the making of nonfiction films, for theaters or television (once it broadened out from travelogues and newsreels), has consistently attracted people of social conscience, very often those on the left.

The late Willard Van Dyke, one of the cameramen on *The River*, gave some interviews that reflect what draws a creative person to work on social documentaries. When he was asked to define social documentary, he said, "It is a film in which the elements of dramatic conflict represent social or political forces rather than individual ones."

No documentary filmmaker expects to get rich on the exhibition of her work. She just wants it to be seen. Those who continue working in this field must be committed to what they are doing. They are the "starving artists" of the movie medium. On the other hand, their moviemaking skills can be useful to the corporate and political bigwigs who run the world. Hence, many of my friends, including most notably Albert Maysles, have done and continue to do commercials and sponsored films for companies like IBM, using profits (the difference between allotted budgets and what it actually costs plus some gravy from print sales) to make the subjects of their choice.

The accessible and relatively easy-to-use video camera and new and efficient digital editing techniques for videotape are rapidly transforming the documentary field, as these developments have already begun to affect the commercial entertainment movie. I was brought up on film and will always prefer it to video, despite the latter's convenience and presumably low cost. An image on film as projected is still far superior to anything that we in this country can project from a videotape—although that is sure to change with the advent of high definition television, which, we are told, is in the offing. But there is something tactile to the handling of film and sound tracks that can never be equaled by some expert in a white shirt twirling knobs.

I remember one young filmmaker (Barry Brown) visiting the Dartmouth campus in the late sixties to show the first feature he had ever directed—*The Way We Live Now*. He had transported this subject in the usual film cans in the rear of his automobile. As writer, director, cameraman, and editor, he clearly felt he had made the movie with his own hands. "Like Michelangelo," he said. "What's in those cans is my work— just as a piece of sculpture was Michelangelo's."

It was a pretentious comparison, but he meant it. The only thing he didn't do, he said, was mix the sound; next time around, he said, he'd do that too.

One student, while respecting Brown's effort, said, "His do-it-yourself mania is a crock. It's like a novelist cutting down a tree with an ax he made so that he could manufacture his own pencils and paper before writing a novel," which leads to a discussion of the avant-garde.

12

+

The Avant-Garde

Having described and praised independent documentary moviemakers for their dedication in the face of economic hardship, I must describe another type of moviemaking that has its gurus and partisans. I refer to the "avant-garde," which can draw enthusiastic audiences to uncomfortable screening rooms in most big cities and at most universities and colleges where movie aficionados congregate.

In my brief history of the movies, I mentioned how the medium itself had a strong attraction in the twenties for artists seeking new forms of self-expression. These included graphic artists like Fernand Léger and Salvador Dalí (who made the celebrated but incomprehensible *Un Chien Andalou* [1929] with Luis Buñuel), photographers like Paul Strand and Ralph Steiner, and poets like Hans Richter and Maya Deren. To philistines like me, who find Michael Snow's *Wave Length* (1967)—a forty-minute zoom shot across an active living room toward a small picture on a far wall—pretentious and boring and ultimately the source of a headache, its enthusiasts would respond that my eyes have been focused on the wrong things too long. It is not easy, they would say with their holier-than-thou posture, to pour new visions into old eyes.

Stan Brakhage, one of the gurus of the avant-garde movement and an excellent film historian, thinks the conventions of narrative sound films are still bound by traditions derived from the novel and theater and that the potentials of the medium for creative expression with the tools at hand have not yet been adequately explored or used. This is not to say that attempts have not been made.

Brakhage himself has attempted to do an abstract interpretation of Dante's *Inferno* by drawing directly on the very large Imax film stock. The result is quite startling and far more stimulating to watch than an earlier work of his called *Sirius Remembered*, which is a crudely shot tribute to his dead dog.

I remember a singular experience with the works of Peter Kubelka, a distinguished avant-garde filmmaker, some of which were presented to a gathering at Dartmouth by a senior concentrating in film studies. One Kubelka film, *Arnulf Rainer* (1960), had no recognizable images at all but consisted entirely of blocks of light—white on black and black on white—for about ten minutes. It was certainly new wine for old taste buds, but the young man who introduced the film went on for more than ten minutes explaining *Arnulf*'s meaning, which went over my head and is now impossible to recall.

The fact that Kubelka was knowledgeable about filmmaking, however, was evident when another of his films—an imaginative documentary, *Unsere Afrikareise* (Our trip to Africa [1966])—was shown later that evening and the audience applauded.

There have been repeated film attempts to deal with the real world in fanciful ways. Francis Thompson did *New York/New York* in the fifties, using prisms and fancy effects, and continued his bizarre style in the multiscreen *To Be Alive*, which was done for the New York World's Fair in the sixties. Shirley Clarke did *Skyscraper* and *Bridge-Go Around*, both visual essays using imaginative techniques to create impressions rather than record reality as it is. But sometimes the visual imagery is used less to show off an environment than to express an idea that does not lend itself too well to simple verbal explanation.

As with documentary filmmakers, many who are drawn to the freewheeling style of avant-garde film or video have social messages to convey that would be totally unacceptable to commercial sponsors. Norman McLaren of the National Film Board of Canada, a distinguished animator, did a stop-motion piece with actors called *Neighbours* (1952) to illustrate the need for nations and people to bury their hatchets over minor disputes. Others simply want to express abstract ideas.

Charles and Ray Eames tried to explain the powers of ten in their film by the same name, *Powers of Ten* (1968). They rejected the idea of using interviews or an authority and did not know how to explain it using pure observation. So they created their own materials, using an extraordinary pullback from a couple making out on the lawn of a park to someplace in outer space and back.

But suppose a filmmaker wants to do an essay on something as abstract as leisure. An imaginative Australian used animation and cutouts to make his point in the film *Leisure* (1976). His story actually begins with a man eking out a living from the soil and indeed working very hard to do so. Rapid transitions then take us to the industrial age, showing man's increased productivity and leading to the question of what he should do with the spare time resulting from that increased productivity.

Very few so-called underground films can be accurately described as documentaries, but many are expressive of ideas and personal statements and many use archival material to make their points—offering a kind of commentary on some aspect of our culture, as pop art does. The people who

make these films are justified in asking that you look at their
work without the usual expectations. They are not especially interested in persuasion, but they want you to think
about a subject, to meditate. Ten minutes on a dripping
faucet or on a woman blinking her eyes or, as Andy Warhol
once did, a single shot of the Empire State Building. These
are unstaged subjects, but what, if anything, do they have to
say? A filmmaker can produce a form of social criticism by
reediting existing film footage. A work by Bruce Conner
called *A Movie* (1958) uses clips from old movies and newsreels to make a comment about violence, the bomb, and
maybe even about movies themselves.

Since documentaries are in something of a rut, dependent
on verité, talking heads, and a kind of didacticism, the
avant-garde can offer a fresh approach that causes an audience to think rather than merely to swallow information.
Film scholars call attention to this category of avant-garde,
which they call structuralist, referring to it as a "cinema of
the mind rather than of the eye." I should also mention the
most recent avant-garde mode in video has led to video dis-
plays in galleries and museums and has created a new breed
of celebrity known as a "video artist," among them Nam
June Paik, Woody Vasulka, Bill Wegman, and Beryl Korot.
On a recent visit to London I was astounded to see that the
celebrated Tate Gallery of Modern Art was devoting an entire room near its entrance to a triptych representing the
video art of an American friend of mine, Bill Viola.

The current infatuation with computer-generated images
and sounds actually originated with avant-garde filmmakers John and Michael Whitney of California, who built their
own computers that were capable of producing ingenious,
often beautiful, color patterns. Moviemaking is, however, a
very ingrown field of endeavor. Moviemakers—many of
them, at any rate—are familiar with the work of other
moviemakers. Hollywood lures many talents away from in-
dependence, but Hollywood big shots, those who hand out

the money to tempt aspiring artists, are also very much in-fluenced by new trends in the media. Michael Eisner, who earned over $50 million in 1995 as head of Disney Enter-prises, may not watch the MTV channel with any degree of enjoyment. But he knows how many million young people *do* watch it devotedly, and aspects of its style have already begun to creep into Disney and Hollywood products.

The disciples of the avant-garde frequently express con-tempt toward commercial moviemaking. As Gene Young-blood puts it:

> Plot, story and what commonly is known as "drama" are the de-vices that enable the commercial entertainer to manipulate his au-dience. The very act of this manipulation, gratifying conditioned needs, is what the films actually are about. . . . The commercial en-tertainer [read *moviemaker*] seeks only to satisfy preconditioned needs for formula stimulus. Entertainment gives us what we want; art gives us what we don't know we want.

Artist Jordan Belsam justifies the absence of form and con-tent in avant-garde works of art:

> If we've tolerated a certain absence of discipline, it has been in favor of freedom through which new language hopefully would be developed. . . . The new cinema [read *the avant-garde*] has emerged as the only aesthetic language to match the envi-ronment in which we live.

The arrogance of the avant-garde filmmaker is sometimes tough to take, but we should remember that these offbeat artists work without a serious concern for commercial gain. We need to subsidize them in some way so that they can continue their work. They currently depend on personal appearances and lec-tures that accompany screenings, on high prices for rentals, and on grants. All these supports are indispensable if they are to con-tinue the experimentation that, in the long run, does indeed exert an impact on filmmaking as a whole.

13

The Future

Most of what I have written in this book pertains to movies made in the United States, since I am most familiar with them. Most of my illustrations are drawn from movies made by the Hollywood industry before 1970. That's because I was a more ardent moviegoer thirty years ago than I am today. Thirty years ago—working as a critic—I recognized moviegoing as my business, but it was also pleasurable.

I am something of a curmudgeon in thinking that we are currently in a quagmire of explicit sex. I can certainly remember when writers like me wished we could use an occasional *damn*, but now that the restrictions are gone, is it necessary to use the word *fuck* a dozen times in a single scene? I am not happy with explicit sex, violence, gore, and a surfeit of street language as elements used to attract and titillate audiences. (In my screenwriting classes, I do not allow toilet scenes of any kind.) I would add that when scatological elements are directed, as they usually are, at what the industry perceives as its primary audience—sixteen-to-twenty-eight-year-olds—and when it is assumed that an audience of popcorn gobblers and coke swizzlers will be bored with anything less than four-letter words, head bashing, shoot-outs, and gore, as well as the sighs, grunts, and exotic exercises of various sexes between the sheets, then the producers are doing a disservice to the fiber of American culture. The American Psychological Association has documented evidence of a link between violence in movies and on TV and violence in real life.

The death knell of the movies has been sounded in the past. The advent of sound was expected by many to put an end to the medium as an art form. The blacklist was expected to put an end to social commentary, and the advent of television was supposed to put an end to theatergoing. The current trend of sex and violence has the potential to reduce movies to comic strips. But it won't.

Suggested Readings

CRITICISM

Arnheim, Rudolf. *Film Essays and Criticism*. Madison: University of Wisconsin Press, 1997.

Kauffmann, Stanley, ed. *American Film Criticism: From the Beginnings to Citizen Kane*. New York: Liveright, 1972.

Rosenbaum, Jonathan. *Placing Movies: The Practice of Film Criticism*. Berkeley: University of California Press.

Staiger, Janet. *Interpreting Films: Studies in the Historical Reception of American Cinema*. Princeton, N.J.: Princeton University Press, 1992.

DOCUMENTARY

Barnouw, Erik. *Documentary: A History of the Non-Fiction Film*. New York: Oxford University Press, 1983.

Barsam, Richard M. *Nonfiction Film: A Critical History*. Bloomington: Indiana University Press, 1992.

Sherman, Sharon R. *Documenting Ourselves: Film, Video, and Culture*. Lexington: University Press of Kentucky, 1998.

HISTORY

Bordwell, David, Janet Staiger, and Kristin Thompson. *The Classical Holly-wood Cinema: Film Style and Mode of Production to 1960*. New York: Columbia University Press, 1985.

Cook, David A. *A History of Narrative Films*. New York: Norton, 1990.

Mast, Gerald. *A Short History of the Movies*. New York: Macmillan, 1986.

Sklar, Robert. *Movie-Made America: A Cultural History of American Movies*. New York: Vintage, 1994.

SCREENWRITING

Engel, Joel, ed. *Screenwriters on Screenwriting: The Best in the Business Discuss Their Craft*. New York: Hyperion, 1995.

Lucey, Paul. *Story Sense: Writing Story and Script for Feature Films and Television*. New York: McGraw-Hill, 1996.

Seger, Linda. *Making a Good Script Great*. Hollywood: Samuel French, 1994.

Stempel, Tom. Framework: *A History of Screenwriting in the American Film*. New York: Continuum, 1988.

STUDIOS

Mordden, Ethan. *The Hollywood Studios: House Style in the Golden Age of the Movies*. New York: Knopf, 1988.

Schatz, Thomas. *The Genius of the System: Hollywood Filmmaking in the Studio Era*. New York: Pantheon, 1988.

Staiger, Janet, ed. *The Studio System*. New Brunswick, N.J.: Rutgers University Press.

THEORY

Andrews, J. Dudley. *The Major Film Theories: An Introduction*. New York: Oxford University Press, 1976.

MacCann, Richard Dyer. *Film: A Montage of Theories*. New York: Dutton, 1966.

Monaco, James. *How to Read a Film: The Art, Technology, Language, History, and Theory of Film and Media*. New York: Oxford University Press, 1981.

Index

About the Author

Maurice Rapf grew up in Hollywood, where his father was one of the founders of M-G-M. He went east and was graduated from Dartmouth College in 1935. He returned to his alma mater in 1966, founded Dartmouth's film studies program, and is now Director Emeritus of Film Studies and an adjunct professor who teaches the course Writing for the Screen every winter term.

Rapf worked as a screenwriter in Hollywood from 1936 to 1947, twice served as secretary of the Screen Writers Guild, and set up the Guild's arbitration system for credits, which is still in effect. He has credit on thirteen movies, his last assignments (for Walt Disney) including *Song of the South*, *So Dear to My Heart*, and *Cinderella*. A victim of the Hollywood blacklist, Rapf left Hollywood in 1947 and never worked there again.

He wrote and/or directed forty or more sponsored films for major U.S. companies, was a film critic for national magazines, and started film study programs at Dartmouth and at Brown. He has three children: Joanna Rapf, a professor at Oklahoma University; Geraldine Rosen, an editor at St. Martin's Press; and William Rapf, head of the art department at Souhegan High School in Amherst, New Hampshire.

Rapf has made his home in Hanover, New Hampshire, location of Dartmouth College, since 1971. "I never intended to write a book about various aspects of the movies or about how they are made. But since I am always amazed at how little movie lovers know about the moviemaking process maybe it's time someone explained it," he says.